EARLS COURT MOTOR SHOW

AN ILLUSTRATED HISTORY

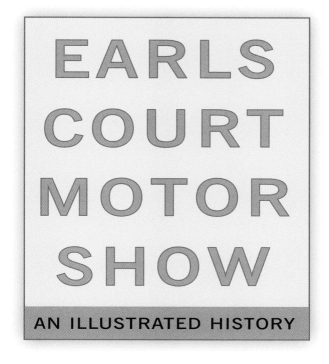

EARLS COURT MOTOR SHOW

AN ILLUSTRATED HISTORY

RUSSELL HAYES

The
History
Press

First published 2016

The History Press
The Mill, Brimscombe Port
Stroud, Gloucestershire, GL5 2QG
www.thehistorypress.co.uk

British Library Cataloguing in Publication Data.
A catalogue record for this book is available from the British Library.

ISBN 978 0 7509 6527 9

Typesetting and origination by The History Press
Printed in China

CONTENTS

FOREWORD

It is hard to believe that the weird art deco structure in Earls Court used to be one of the most glamorous places in the world. Stuffed with celebrities, slinky sports cars and cigar-chomping tycoons, it was a cathedral to car worship and a glittering social event in London's calendar. Wide-eyed punters would queue for hours and jostle ten deep to catch a glimpse of a new Jag XK120, E-Type, Rolls Silver Shadow or Morris Mini Minor. Every year I made the pilgrimage, armed with a vast carrier bag to fill with glossy brochures. Earls Court is where I saw Richard Burton and Elizabeth Taylor, Peter Sellers and Diana Rigg, and in 1971 the models on the TVR stand were completely naked. Earls Court was always sexy, glitzy and unmissable.

These were the days when the global motor industry was at its zenith, filling the halls with Ferraris, Maseratis, Lamborghinis, ACs and Jensens. Caramel-skinned playboys with girlfriends in mink coats would sign cheques on the stands for Daytonas and Miuras while sipping champagne. I soon learnt that if I wore a suit and washed my hair I too could talk my way past the uniformed commissionaire and rub shoulders with the millionaires. For a car-crazy teenager, Earls Court was a temple of surreal wonder where stars and cars glinted like diamonds and the world seemed safe, solid and enormously prosperous. That this politically incorrect shrine to automotive excess couldn't continue forever was inevitable, but we must never forget how much pleasure, glamour and hope it gave to so many people. I'm proud to have been one of them.

Quentin Willson
Motoring Journalist

ACKNOWLEDGEMENTS

With thanks to The History Press for grasping my idea and Amy Rigg for her support and answers to many questions. Thanks too to Quentin Willson for his encouragement from the start.

Contributors

Thanks to: Tony Ball, John Baumber, Richard Bremner, Harry Calton, Bob Dilley and Geoff Howard, who shared their time and show memories; Ben Klemenszon of *Classic American* magazine (www.classic-american.com), Steve Miles and Geoff Carverhill for their American car knowledge; and James Peill, curator of the Goodwood Collection, for some fact-checking.

Archive Material

Many thanks to Richard Wiltshire and Joanne Ruff at the City of London Corporation London Metropolitan Archives (LMA) for access to the Earls Court and Olympia archive, and to Belinda Liversedge, communications manager at Olympia Management Services Limited for help and permission to reproduce material.

Thanks also to: Will Carleton at the Press Photo History Project (www.pressphotohistory.com); Simon Flavin and the team at Mirrorpix (www.mirrorpix.com) for digging out some fine images; Mark Dowd and the team at TopFoto (www.topfoto.co.uk); Kevin Wood at LAT Photographic

(Haymarket); Damian Kimberley and the staff at the Coventry History Centre for access to the Rootes and Society of Motor Manufacturers and Traders (SMMT) archives; and SMMT communications manager Janet Wilkinson for help and permission to reproduce the show catalogues.

Very many thanks to: Andrew Duerden at Vauxhall Heritage for generous provision of images; Giles Chapman for rapid archive photo provision (www.gileschapman.com); Angela Willis, curator of the Caravan Club collection at the National Motor Museum; Robert Wine, BP Group press officer, for information and the image for BP Build-a-Car; Shahin Armin for the 1970s colour images (www.paykanhunter.com); and Bob Clare of the Panther Car Club (www.panthercarclub.com).

1 MAKING AN EXHIBITION 1887–1939

Britons got a taste for grand exhibitions well before the motorcar. The Great Exhibition of 1851 in Joseph Paxton's huge iron-and-glass 'Crystal Palace' in Hyde Park was an immense success in showing the skills and goods of a colonial power at its peak. Although designed as a temporary structure, it was rebuilt in 1852 in Sydenham, South London, and inspired the Royal Agricultural Hall in Islington, which opened in 1862.

THE FIRST BRITISH MOTOR SHOWS AND OLYMPIA

The transition from horse and carriage to horseless carriage was cautious. There had been steam-powered buses in the early half of the century and enough smaller steam-powered vehicles for the second Locomotives Act of 1865 to restrict speed to 4mph in the country and 2mph in town, with somebody walking in front with a red flag.

The 1890s marked lift-off for the gasoline internal combustion engine, although motoring was still a very specialist interest with sections of the population decidedly fearful of these new contraptions. In 1895 there were about two dozen petrol-driven cars on British roads and, although just two British companies were offering to build cars at the end of that year, the number was about to explode. German and French manufacturers were speeding ahead and their products were popular imports.

The first British motor show took place at an agricultural showground in Tunbridge Wells in 1895, organised by Sir David Salomons, founder of the Self-Propelled Traffic Association. Just four cars were shown, all of them French but able to go as fast as they could on private land. The event attracted favourable newspaper support for a higher speed limit, according to motoring historian Nick Georgano in *Britain's Motor Industry: The First Hundred Years*.

The year 1886 had been a landmark one for the car. Carl Benz, regarded as the inventor of the purpose-designed petrol-engined car, introduced the Benz Patent Motor Car. Ten years later, in 1896, the Locomotives Act was amended to increase the maximum speed to 14mph and banish the man with the red flag. The fastest recorded speed that year was 10mph.

Meanwhile, a purpose-built exhibition centre for London took shape on ground in West Kensington along the Hammersmith Road. The owners of the Agricultural Hall in Islington set up the National Agricultural Hall Company in 1884 to build Britain's largest exhibition space to take its military and livestock shows to a much greater audience near the West End of London. Its vast iron-framed roof, designed by architect Henry Edward Coe, had a 170ft clear span and is still standing today.

The National Agricultural Hall opened in December 1886 but is now known by the name it was given in 1946: Kensington Olympia, or simply Olympia. Despite hosting some hugely popular circus shows, a water-filled recreation of Venice and a few large exhibitions,

Between 1896 and 1906 the Earls Court grounds hosted London's first big wheel, which was 300ft high and took 1,200 passengers at a time. Here it towers above the 1906 Austro-Hungarian exhibition. (Olympia/LMA)

Olympia lurched from receivership to liquidation as its gigantic spectacles ran over budget and exhibitors chopped and changed, with three owners in its first ten years. For a far fuller account of entertainments in the early days of Olympia it's well worth tracking down a copy of John Glanfield's out-of-print book *Earls Court and Olympia: From Buffalo Bill to the 'Brits'*.

In 1896 London saw motor exhibitions at Crystal Palace and the Imperial Institute, and over Christmas Olympia hosted the International Motor Show and Cycle Tournament, its first motor show, but did not have enough cars to avoid sharing space with other exhibitors. A 'Cycling and Motor Car Exhibition' is also documented for 1897.

Of course, Britain was not alone in embracing the motor show and greater car-producing nations in Europe were joining in. In 1897 Berlin hosted the Internationale Automobil-Ausstellung. The Automobile Club de France, founded in 1895, created the first Exposition internationale de l'automobile, du cycle et des sports in Paris, in 1898. The first Turin Motor Show was in 1900; Geneva in 1905. In the twentieth century these names would vie with London for status in the minds of car makers and writers, if not the public; Frankfurt took over from Berlin and Hanover in 1951.

Centres of British car manufacturing were growing fast, especially in the Midlands. Car ownership was still the preserve of the modern-thinking aristocracy but middle-class customers such as

Britain's first manufacturer-supported motor show was held at London's Olympia, November 1905. (Mirrorpix)

doctors were joining them. The time for an industry-backed large-scale motor show had come, and Frederick Simms, a British engineer, created the Society of Motor Manufacturers and Traders (SMMT) in 1902 as a trade body to bring together Britain's growing but disparate motor industry and promote its interests at home and abroad. At first its principal aim was to exercise control over motor shows and the first SMMT-backed exhibition was held at Crystal Palace in January 1903. With more than 180 exhibitors in an area of 87,000 sq.ft, the show catalogue proclaimed it the largest motor show in the world. There was money to be made from exhibition space for motorcars even in those early days. Also in 1903 the Earls Court grounds hosted the Stanley Automobile Exhibition (after the

Stanley Cycle Club) and the Royal Agricultural Hall in Islington also offered a motor show.

Frederick Payne, Olympia's managing director between 1886 and 1912, made a decisive move away from spectacles by freeing up every inch of floor space possible for the growing market in trade exhibitions, ripping out the arena seating in 1904 and installing a new concrete floor. It worked, with a regular calendar of trade shows fillings its halls until in February 1905 the SMMT was persuaded to bring its growing show to Olympia. It was such a success that another was held in November.

As show organisers the SMMT became and remained a force to be reckoned with. As John Glanfield recounts, one condition of

Seen in November 1936, the Earls Court exhibition centre was built over eighteen months. It used 24,000 tons of cement, 120,000 tons of shingle and 80,000cu. yards of concrete. (Olympia/LMA)

the show coming to Olympia was that nobody else could exhibit motorised transport there without its consent and it extended its reach to boats and aeroplanes, mixing both with buses and lorries for the 1907 Commercial Motor Vehicle and Boat Exhibition, a combination that didn't last.

By 1913 the British motor industry was building 25,000 cars and 9,000 commercial vehicles, placing it third in the world for vehicle production. During the First World War, Olympia was at first requisitioned as a temporary prison camp for German nationals before becoming home to the Royal Army Clothing Depot. The Motor Show returned in 1919 and demanded ever more space. There was an overflow to White City for three years until adjoining buildings were demolished for a new hall completed in 1923. The Motor Show remained an annual fixture at Olympia until 1936, after which it lost out to the impressive new Earls Court exhibition space to its south.

EARLS COURT SPECTACLES, 1887–1936

While Olympia struggled to make ends meet in its early days, a lot of fun could be had a few blocks south at Earls Court on an awkward triangular parcel of West London land hemmed in by houses and railway lines.

The area name of Earls Court comes from the De Vere family, who were granted the Manor of Kensington after the Norman Conquest in 1066; the heads of the family held the title of Earl of Oxford until 1703. In the nineteenth century the Earl of Zetland owned the freehold of the land, and he laid the foundation stone of Olympia in 1885.

Earls Court was transformed from rural land to a densely packed London suburb after the building of the Metropolitan District Railway station in 1865–69. Four lines ran through cuttings and sidings on

Heating was provided by water electrically heated in seven 45ft-long storage tanks, the same diameter as a tube train. (Olympia/LMA)

the railway-owned 23-acre site. It was and still is a major interchange of West London transport, but as the land was awkwardly shaped it had two stations, at Old Brompton Road (West Brompton) and Warwick Road (Earls Court) to deliver and despatch vast numbers of people.

The first spectacle to take place there was the vision of Yorkshire engineer John Robinson Whitley who teamed up with American backers for an American Exhibition of arts and industry scheduled for May 1886. This slipped to 1887 as doubts grew about Whitley's support, but his masterstroke was to sign up Colonel William Frederic 'Buffalo Bill' Cody the legendary horseman who in avenging Colonel Custer's 'last stand' had killed Indian Chief Yellow Hand. Cody turned his famous exploits into Buffalo Bill's Wild West Show with hundreds of real Indians and cowboys plus the equally famous sharpshooter Annie Oakley.

The bleak Earls Court site was transformed with railway shed-like exhibition halls, an arena seating 20,000 and painted hoardings concealing the railways, which ran in cuttings across the site. A rollercoaster railway and water chute were added but Bill somewhat overshadowed the exhibition his show was meant to support. By the time it closed in October over 2 million visitors had come to Earls Court. Buffalo Bill returned in 1892.

A period of disrepair followed as Earls Court tried to find its way but it was transformed in the 1890s by Imre Kiralfy, who had masterminded Olympia's shows, which would run for months. Taking a twenty-one-year lease, his first Earls Court venture was the 1895 Empire of India show. He built the 5,000-seat Empress Theatre in 1896 and a 300ft-high great wheel, capable of carrying 1600 visitors, which was a major attraction between 1896 and 1906.

The ground floor contained a hidden swimming pool which could be lowered or raised by section but was only briefly used as a pool. Seating on the upper levels could be provided by two-tier structures on wheels. (Olympia/LMA)

Earls Court Exhibition Bldg.
Progress Photo Date 19-6-37
HEGEMAN HARRIS CO., Inc., Builders.
Swimming - Pool.

As the First World War broke, the theatre and other buildings on the Earls Court site were requisitioned in late 1914 as a refugee-processing centre, then an ammunition store. Post-1919 peacetime, barring the occasional circus or fair, the big shows and exhibitions did not return. It became a store for unwanted buses and the buildings deteriorated. By 1934 Earls Court Grounds Ltd was in receivership.

THE EARLS COURT EXHIBITION CENTRE TAKES SHAPE

The impetus to use the land for something permanent came from the need to provide a regular home for the ever-expanding British Industries Fair (one staged in London, the other in Birmingham since 1920), a Great Exhibition for the twentieth century with only

British and colonial producers of goods exhibiting. It was a matter of government concern and national pride, with trade fairs booming in Europe, notably Germany.

Earls Court Ltd was formed in 1935, chaired by Sir Ralph Glyn, who remained involved until 1972. Having obtained a ninety-nine-year lease of the land from the London Passenger Transport Board and having secured the British Industries Fair plus the Ideal Home Exhibition and the Motor Show from Olympia, it moved fast to lay its plans. As John Glanfield put it: 'Earls Court was never intended simply to compete with Olympia. It was planned to dominate what its management and workplace called "the village hall" up the road.'

US firm Hegeman-Harris Co. Inc., which had contracted for New York's Rockefeller Centre was given the £1.5m project. It hired architect C. Howard Crane from Detroit, Michigan to design the new exhibition building, which bore art deco flourishes reminiscent of his specialisation in movie and entertainment theatres. Crane had been London-based

At its 'practical completion', on 22 July 1937, Earls Court was claimed to be the largest entertainment and exhibition centre in the world. The Warwick Road entrance has yet to gain its giant Earls Court lettering. (Olympia/LMA)

since his Detroit work dried up following the 1929 Great Depression, and would go on to design further buildings in the capital.

Design engineer for the project was L.G. Mouchel & Partners. In 1910 the company had designed the Michelin Building in nearby Chelsea, the first two chimneys of Battersea power station in 1921 and was a specialist in reinforced concrete; this was to be one of the largest reinforced concrete structures in the world.

It was a sensational specification for the time, an exhibition centre covering 9 acres of the 12-acre triangular site with a roof span that could enclose Trafalgar Square. The structure was planned to be Europe's biggest by volume. The specification included plans for 450,000 sq.ft of column-free exhibition space on two levels to accommodate 23,000 visitors at any one time and a hidden 200 x 100ft swimming pool beneath a retractable 760-ton concrete floor. The upper floors could be divided into three sections so that four exhibitions could be held simultaneously.

What had started as steam railway lines in cuttings and tunnels were now even busier electrified tube line routes on each edge of the triangle. To liberate the maximum amount of floor space, two sets of double tracks and two singles had to be crossed. The two District lines which ran through cuttings on two sides of the triangle were enclosed to provide access roads around the building, the covering supported on sixty concrete bridges. Car parking space for 2,000 cars was provided on the land to the south of the new building across the railway lines behind the building, joined by a covered walkway.

Around 1,000 beams supported the building, carrying loads of 2,500 tons each. Those directly over railway lines sat on portals or bridges, and the main exhibition floor had to be suspended 15ft above ground level to provide a clear basement above the tracks.

Oscar Faber's consultancy – Faber was also a pioneer in the use of reinforced concrete – designed the ventilation system. The air was claimed to be washed and heated and kept at an 'equable

The giant complex seen from the air in August 1937, with the Empress Hall to the left, Earls Court car park crossing the railway tracks, the Brompton Road entrance and main building. (IMAGNO/ Austrian Archives (S) Topfoto)

temperature' to stop visitors feeling tired. Eight ventilation plants on the roof blew air downwards, with extraction via side ducts and slots in the false ceiling.

There was no natural light and the artificial lighting could be adjusted to suit each exhibition. Every exhibition stand could be provided with cold water, drainage, gas, electricity and telephone, and dust chutes carried rubbish away to an incinerator. Lorries could be driven onto the relevant floor via three huge lorry lifts. There were five lifts each for visitors and service as well as six escalators.

The swimming pool could be put into action by lowering three sections of the centre ground floor and each could be raised independently up to 5ft above floor level in twenty minutes. This opened up a host of possible water features for exhibitions, not least the Boat Show from 1960, with boats sitting in a real harbour. It was little used as a swimming pool but one early entertainment was

the Aqua Show in 1948: a month-long 'stage and water spectacle' starring Johnny Weissmuller of Tarzan fame and Esther Williams. Before filling or draining it the water authorities had to approve as it held 2¼ million gallons and took four days to fill. Filling or emptying could only be done at night to prevent overloading local services. A 1978 campaign to revive the 'lost pool' for the 1982 World Swimming Championships did not succeed.

The building could be divided into three concert halls 'Warwick', 'Richmond' and 'Philbeach' named after neighbouring roads and areas. There were four restaurants, five tea lounges and twenty-five snack bars.

An average workforce of 3,000 men built Earls Court. Hegeman-Harris was given fourteen months until Christmas day 1936 to hand the finished building over, but it overshot to 22 July 1937 due to delayed steel deliveries. These caused havoc with those exhibitions

The orderly rows and signage of the first Earls Court Motor Show ,14–23 October 1937, set a pattern followed for decades. (IMAGNO/Austrian Archives (S) Topfoto)

that had planned to be the hall's first customers. The BIF had to be hastily moved to the former Olympic showground at White City and the first Earls Court event was a Chocolate and Confectionary Exhibition.

Nonetheless, this was a significant new venue, as the owners proclaimed: 'Earls Court is destined to play a significant part in our national life.'

Refurbished and renamed, the Empress Hall was leased from Earls Court Ltd and adapted for ice skating, and new buildings erected for an ice-making plant and a ventilation and heating plant. A pedestrian bridge and roadway linked it to the main site. The ice shows lasted until 1958, it was demolished in 1960 and the twenty-eight-storey Empress State building was built on the Lillie Road site in 1962.

THE FIRST TWO EARLS COURT MOTOR SHOWS

Car use on British roads had leapt from 8,465 registrations in 1904 to 1½ million by 1935 and the 'big six' domestic manufacturers dominating the market were Morris, Austin, Standard, Humber, Ford and Vauxhall, the last two being British subsidiaries of American companies.

The first Earls Court Motor Show opened at its new home on 14 October 1937 and closed ten days later. There were fifty-seven British exhibitors, five German, four Italian, five French and one Belgian. It took the same scope as the Olympia shows, sections divided into Private Motor Cars, Carriage Work, Motor Boats and Marine Engines, Caravans and Trailers on the ground floor with garage equipment, accessories and tyres on the first.

Two women pose decorously in the boot of the new Triumph Dolomite at the exhibition on 13 October 1937. (Mirrorpix)

Ladies were given free admission if accompanied by gentlemen for three reasons, said the *Daily Express*: there was more room than in Olympia, men often needed advice from their womenfolk when buying cars and there were more women drivers than ever.

The motoring press duly filed their reports on the new cars and the new venue. *Motorsport* magazine (founded in 1924) was disappointed to find that, having arrived later during press day, all the new car-parking space had been filled, and the motoring press continued to moan about a lack of parking for decades to come.

Nonetheless, once inside, *Motorsport*'s correspondent was quite happy, writing in the November 1937 edition:

The stone floors and ample ventilation prove an excellent antidote to even the most susceptible 'Olympia heads' and the bareness of the stands, with their conventional layout, even to the makers' signs, is compensated by the freedom of movement made possible – only in isolated cases were these stands roped round – by the general sense of light and airiness, and particularly by the ease with which one could locate a stand from a glance at the high-slung overhead names.

It naturally tended to enthuse over the performance cars and it was a glorious time for fast cars for the wealthy. The 5-litre Mercedes 500K had sold to the Sultan of Jahore before the show started but there were still Bugattis, Delahayes and Lagondas to choose from. Other sporting attractions included a new streamlined coupé bodyshell for the SS 100 sports car from the Swallow Sidecar Company, designed by its founder William Lyons. The company had been using the name Jaguar SS for its sports cars since 1935 and would drop the SS tag after the war to become simply Jaguar. The Type 328 Frazer-Nash-BMW (a German car with a British badge) had been tested at 103mph and a 100mph top speed was not unusual for the most expensive performance cars.

On the cheaper British sports car side, the new Morgan 4/4 sports car continued the departure of the Malvern marque from the three-wheelers of its beginnings, setting a style that is still visible in its 2016 cars. Exhibiting its T-Type sports cars, the MG Car Company had been formed in 1930 with its origins in sporting Morris cars (MG for Morris Garages). It grew rapidly to produce sports cars and sporting saloons, with 1937 marking its best pre-war production of 2,901 cars.

Bringing up the affordable side of motoring, the very first Fiat 500 had been introduced in 1937 and was nicknamed *Topolino*, 'little mouse' in Italian. Its British counterpart, the tiny 747cc Austin Seven, had been produced in various forms since 1922, was re-bodied and imitated across the world, and ended production in 1939 with almost 300,000 built.

A notable absentee from the new venue was Ford, as between 1932 and 1937 it hired the Royal Albert Hall to display its entire range of cars and commercial vehicles in the auditorium, with the loggia or boxes acting as sales offices. The new model for 1937 was the Eight. Since 1934 Ford had held on to the honour of selling the cheapest car in Britain, the Model Y Popular.

Prince George, Duke of Kent, opened the 1938 Earls Court Motor Show and a special guest plus car was Captain George Eyston, who had broken the world speed record that September in his streamlined Thunderbolt, its twin V12 Rolls-Royce aero engines taking it to nearly 346mph at Bonneville Salt Flats in America. Britain was in the grip of land-speed-record fever between 1937 and 1939, with fierce competition between two Englishmen, Eyston and John Cobb, with one sometimes wresting the record from the other in a matter of days.

A very great deal slower, the new Morris Ten looked conventional but its all-in-one unitary body structure with no separate chassis was thoroughly modern, following the example of Citroën and Vauxhall.

Although Britain was preparing itself for a further war with Germany, there was still much enthusiasm for German cars and admiration for the nation's racing prowess and resources, although by now largely supplied by the Nazis. Before the show there had been visiting racing teams from Auto Union and Mercedes, but Auto Union had its cars impounded.

Despite the new building being warmly received, by July 1939 Earls Court Ltd was in receivership – and yet Olympia was suffering through loss of events to its new rival. As war threatened, Earls Court

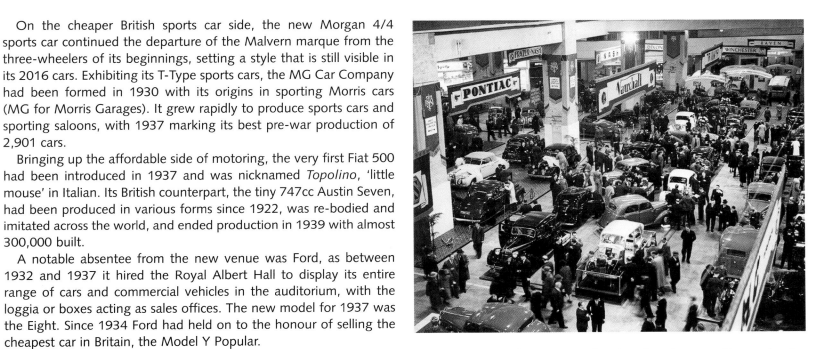

A small selection of caravans and trailers shared space with cars, boats and marine engines. (Vauxhall Heritage)

events for the remainder of 1939 started to be cancelled. Followers of Sir Oswald Mosley's British Union of Fascists gathered on 16 July and filled its seats (it was to be banned in 1940), the Salvation Army cancelled its farewell to its founder General Booth on 2 September and war was declared the next day. There was to be no 1939 Motor Show.

Motorsport poignantly reflected, 'Definitely, we shall miss going to Earls Court. The Motor Show, whether at Olympia, or Olympia and White City, or, as it now is, or would have been, at the newer Earl's Court building, brings annually a pleasing mixture of experiences.'

Earls Court's vast space was put to an unusual wartime use: the inflation and testing of the 'blimps' of the London air defence balloon barrage, while a wind tunnel – built in secret in the Empress Hall – saw testing of the first jet engines. Olympia became an internment camp and the headquarters of the Free French Army.

2 THE ROAD AHEAD 1946–49

Earls Court was de-requisitioned in late 1946, pockmarked by shrapnel and blackened by pollution. Its management company, Earls Court Ltd, was still in receivership and struggled to rebuild its roster of shows. In May 1947 it played host to the British Industries Fair, while the Empress Hall hosted the boxing, gymnastic, weightlifting and wrestling events of the summer 1948 London Olympic Games. A Motor Show was announced for both 1946 and 1947 but postponed so as not to 'provide any distractions from the development of post-war designs and a concentration on Export trade', the 1949 show guide revealed.

The majority of Britain's car factories had come through the war relatively unscathed even though they had been devoted to military vehicle and aircraft production. From 1936 extra plants called shadow factories had been built in the anticipation of conflict and these now provided extra capacity for private cars.

Ford at Dagenham – considered a model factory – resumed production almost seamlessly, with 31,974 vehicles built in 1946. It was the mightiest car plant in Europe with a capacity of 200,000. However the Nuffield Organisation – chiefly Morris – still dominated British motor manufacturing, with 41,182 Morris cars sold in 1946 (model year August 1945–July 1946). Next in terms of size were Austin, then Standard (which bought Triumph in 1944), Rootes and the other US-owned car maker Vauxhall. The first British-built Vauxhall had appeared in 1903 but the company was bought out by General Motors in 1925.

This was the time of the motor barons. The making of British cars and commercial vehicles was largely in the hands of a small and powerful collection of knighted men. Standard was Sir John Black, Morris was Lord Nuffield, Rootes was Sir William 'Billy' Rootes and his brother Reginald and Sir Leonard Lord (knighted 1954) ruled the Austin empire. It was their characters as much as market forces which shaped their model ranges and the fate of their companies, sometimes for the worse.

Aside from loss of life, the other price of victory was a shattered economy. Rationing of most resources was set to continue into the next decade and survival for the political parties depended on how well they managed shortages. Private 'pleasure' motoring had disappeared during the war, restricted by the issue of ration coupons, which you applied for and were given according to use. If you had to use your car for work you got more coupons depending on the distance travelled. Petrol theft was common.

At the start of the war, private motorists had been limited to 200 miles a month to save petrol, but from 1942, unless you were in a special position, you could not buy petrol at all. Many owners put their cars on blocks in the garage if they had one. In the early years of peacetime the petrol supply wavered in the face of short-term need. The basic ration was then withdrawn altogether in autumn 1947 on the basis that the government needed to save £5 million. When it returned the following year, private motorists were still restricted to fuel for approximately 3 miles a day up until 1949 and

The Standard Vanguard was the first new British mass-market family saloon on the market in 1947 and the sole model the company made until 1953. (Giles Chapman Picture Library)

had to use poor-quality 'pool' petrol. During the war, brands had disappeared and the previous three grades of fuel were blended and shared out. Motorists complained that 1946 pool petrol was of even poorer quality than the 1939 mix, and car engine designers had to look abroad to find petrol good enough to test their more efficient designs and higher compression ratios.

The reforming 1945–51 Labour government intervened in the motor industry as much as any other. The country needed to earn foreign currency to buy imported food and raw materials. 'Export or die' was a Ministry of Information slogan which became a mantra. Consumer goods were a priority for export markets, and that certainly meant cars. Half of car production had to be for export and in 1947 this was raised to 75 per cent. As European factories were slower to rebuild, Britain had a short-term lead supplying its colonial markets such as Australia and South Africa.

Steel was rationed to each carmaker according to their potential to generate export orders – not by their size – and they were also encouraged to concentrate on single-model ranges.

Sir Stafford Cripps, former Minister of Aircraft Production, became President of the Board of Trade and announced at the November 1945 SMMT annual dinner that car makers should produce a tough, good-looking car for roads and journeys rougher and longer than little England. Because manufacturers hadn't considered exports a great deal, pre-war cars were ill suited for bashing down dirt roads and had gained a reputation for disintegration, which stuck. There were no motorways in Britain until the late 1950s so British cars, with small free-revving engines, would expire undertaking American freeway driving.

While demand for new cars gradually built up in export markets, the home market was starved. British motorists were often actively prevented from being able to buy a new car by a swingeing domestic purchase tax rate of 33.3 per cent. In 1948 an Austin Devon, the smallest model in the range, was £362 but British purchase tax added £101. For cars with a basic purchase price above £1,000 the tax was doubled. The latter was halved in 1950 only to be restored in 1951 when the country rearmed for the Korean War.

The Jowett Javelin from Bradford had many advanced features and followed the style of European cars such as Lancias. (Giles Chapman Picture Library)

A thriving black market in new cars sprang up and the government introduced a covenant that compelled owners of new cars to keep them for at first at least one year rather than sell them on at a profit straight away. Used cars cost more than new.

THE NEW WAVE

While most of the new cars offered for sale in the early post-war years were mildly updated 1939 designs, car makers had been allowed to spend some time during the war developing new models thanks to an agreement brokered by the SMMT, and by October 1944 fifty-six firms had been allowed to go ahead. The late 1940s brought an outpouring of new British designs, principally four-door compact saloons.

With no Motor Show in 1947, Standard's Sir John Black garnered maximum publicity for the all-new Standard Vanguard in July 1947, its name recalling a famous warship. Standard had followed Cripps's

entreaties for an attractive car for export and a single model-range, and in return received dollars to buy machine tools and low rent on a shadow factory. Black scrapped the pre-war car range of the 8, 12 and 14 saloons in favour of the Vanguard, although at first British motorists could only buy the old models while the new car was export only.

The Vanguard's 2,088cc overhead-valve engine was already in use on the Ferguson tractor, which Standard assembled. Standard's head of body engineering Walter Belgrove had spent hours sketching Plymouths outside the American Embassy in London and the Vanguard's fastback shape was obviously transatlantic but looked instantly modern compared to the competition. Such was the excitement over this new British car that it made it on to newsreels and the BBC. Production started in 1948 and it sold well with 185,000 of the first series built until 1952. It was meant to be a world car, yet, in its rush to market, had only been tested on the rough roads of Wales, according to Nick Georgano's *Complete Encyclopaedia of Motor Cars*, the engineers only able to guess at

The Jaguar XK120 was the dream car of the 1947 show and an instant success. The following decade saw a meteoric rise for the company. (Newspress)

the stresses the suspension and dust sealing would be put under on a South African dirt road or even Belgian pavé. There was less excuse for this type of error from 1948, when the newly established Motor Industry Research Association opened a test track in Warwickshire complete with arduous surfaces.

A bigger sensation of 1947 came from an even smaller manufacturer than Standard. In May 1947 the Bradford car maker Jowett (est. 1906) launched the Javelin, a roomy four-door saloon with a novel horizontally opposed 'flat four' engine of 1.5 litres. Its fastback shape was more graceful than the Vanguard and it gained a reputation for being well engineered, winning its category 1949 Monte Carlo Rally and the fastest touring car in Belgium's 24 Hours of Spa race. Road testers marvelled at its ability to cruise at 70mph and reasonable fuel consumption.

The Javelin also used a relatively new method of construction which was to become the norm by the end of the following decade; rather than being attached to a separate chassis, its steel body panels were welded together to form a single 'unitary' body shell

or monocoque which was lighter and stronger but more vulnerable to rust. Vauxhall had been a British pioneer with the 1937 10hp. Morris followed in 1939 with its 10 and Hillman with the 1940 Minx, but unitary construction did not feature across their ranges until the 1950s.

For aesthetics, Britain looked to America for a vision of a prosperous nation of car owners, and with ever-increasing size and ornamentation American cars were exhibited at Earls Court to gawp at. The British motoring press were reliably snooty about such vulgarity but American styling trends and brighter colours influenced most popular domestic cars, albeit scaled down.

Good examples, new in 1947, were the Austin A40 Devon and Dorset, two medium-sized 1200cc saloons with four and two doors respectively and rounded styling reminiscent of a 1941 Chevrolet. At the other end of the scale, Austin introduced its A125 six-cylinder Sheerline limousine in 1947, made by its own coachbuilder, the London firm of Vanden Plas, which it had bought in 1946.

THE 1948 SHOW

It was against this backdrop of hardship and ambition that the SMMT decided to resume the Earls Court Motor Show in October 1948, ten years after the last one. On Wednesday 28th the show was opened by HRH the Duke of Gloucester. The motor industry was enjoying a whole new status.

There were forty-five car exhibitors, fifty-five makes, twenty-one exhibitors in the coachwork section, 251 in the accessories and components section, and seventy-five in the equipment section. This was not quite enough to fill the ground floor of the main hall. As before, the left-hand part was the marine section with forty-six motorboat exhibitors and eighteen in the caravan and trailer division at the rear of the hall. Car makers made up the centre section and the coachbuilders largely occupied the right-hand side. The floor plan reflected the state of the world's auto industry. French, American and Italian manufacturers were present but German makes would be on the banned list until the 1950s. The show was open from 10 a.m. to 9 p.m. and admission prices, depending on the day and time, ranged from 2s 6d to 5s.

Once through the doors at Warwick Road, almost bang in the middle of the show were those comfortingly tweedy and successful Austin 'Counties' cars, the Dorset and Devon, were joined by their bigger brother the A70 Hampshire in the 2.1-litre class. But all eyes were on the Austin A90 Atlantic, Birmingham's interpretation of what they thought the American market would like: a two-door convertible with swooping lines, rear wheel spats and plated streaks down the bonnet that aped a Pontiac and interior instruments with a gold finish. The Atlantic was built on the Hampshire's chassis: its four-cylinder engine enlarged to 2.6 litres with a manual column gear change. The British audience marvelled at the electro-hydraulically powered hood.

Despite this domestic enthusiasm, it failed to please American buyers. For $2,460 they could have had a V8 engine and automatic transmission. Instead the Austin 'Four' struggled to pull such a heavy car and the narrow track and inadequate brakes didn't help.

All the same Austin ensured it did break a record (always good publicity even if there was no other competition for said record) for driving non-stop for seven days and seven nights at over 70mph for 11,875 miles around the Indianapolis race circuit in April 1949,

After a surprise debut at the 1948 show, Morris Minor Low Light Sedans make their way off the production line for export at Morris's Cowley factory in March 1949. (Mirrorpix)

In 1948 Hillman displayed a 'Ghost Minx' with see-through Perspex panels that showed its construction when illuminated. (Rootes, courtesy of Coventry History Centre)

achieving sixty-three speed and endurance records; but to no avail in the showrooms. Neither the records nor a $1,000 price but helped sales. Aimed back at the British market, the Atlantic convertible was joined by a fabric-topped hardtop version in 1950, improved brakes in 1951, but it was an expensive curiosity in its native land and ceased production in 1952. Of a total production of around 10,000 cars, a lamentable 350 were sold in the US. The engine, however, was to achieve greater success in Austin-Healey sports cars.

Austin's deadly rival and eventual partner Morris had, on the other hand, got its product exactly right at the 1948 show with the debut of the Morris Minor, which was to become a highly significant car. It had held back its introduction until the show for maximum impact.

According to Jon Pressnell's definitive *Morris: The Cars and the Company*, the Minor had begun as a smaller Fiat 500-sized concept in 1941 but by 1944 was in development as a larger car, the 'Mosquito'. All of its design was the work of the highly talented

Alec Issigonis, who went on to design the Mini. Being both of unitary construction and boasting independent front suspension with rack-and-pinion steering, the Minor was a truly modern car with excellent handling. The styling was also a good interpretation of American trends. Had time and funds allowed, its look would have been more advanced, with concealed headlamps and an all-new flat-four engine design. However, the first MM (as it was known internally) Series Minor carried through the 918cc side-valve engine from the pre-war Morris 8, which it was to supplant. 'Because of the lack of new models of the popular and economical 8hp cars which fit so well into small garages and are so handy on congested narrow roads, the new Morris Minor is likely to receive an ovation,' *The Autocar* anticipated.

Despite the Nuffield Organisation's doubts about what it considered a dangerously radical new car (Lord Nuffield hated it, and there was still a waiting list for the 8), the Minor was an immediate

THE ARISTOCRACY

Unsurprisingly, socialist austerity Britain was a difficult place to be for luxury carmakers. In its review of the carriage-work section of the show, *The Autocar* summed it up: '1948 is not a moment in history when the construction of luxurious town carriages for the nobility and gentry, or even simply peoples' cars for the working man, is given much encouragement.'

At the first Earls Court show in 1937 Rolls-Royce had exhibited its chassis with bodywork by Hooper, Barker, Thrupp & Maberley and Windover but it knew that eventually it would have to move away from the traditional practice of producing a chassis and running gear upon which coachbuilders would build different body styles with bespoke details for their wealthy customers and offer the option of its own steel body, especially to increase production and hence exports.

Bentley, which Rolls-Royce had owned since 1933 to produce more sporting and slightly cheaper luxury transport, was first to offer a standard steel-bodied saloon (with a shell from Pressed Steel Co.) and the Mk VI was introduced in 1946. In 1949 a Rolls-Royce version, the Silver Dawn, was produced to appeal to the American market more used to its name than Bentley's.

Rolls meanwhile did its bit for standardisation by offering its Silver Wraith chassis with only one 4887cc engine. In 1948 its show stand featured a four-door sports saloon by Park Ward (Rolls-Royce had its own directors on the board), touring limousine by Hooper, a Sedanca de Ville (four doors and a removable top over the chauffeur) by H.J. Mulliner and a four-seat drophead coupé by Gurney Nutting. On the Bentley stand the standard steel sports saloon was also joined by coach-built versions from three of the above.

Being much smaller than mass-market manufacturers, coach building firms struggled to rebuild their staff (and their skills) after the war and the cost of having a special body on a chassis of your choice had rocketed. A special body in a Rolls-Royce was between £1,500 and £2,000, so with purchase tax a Rolls for an English customer was around £6,000. With costs and increasingly standardised bodyshells, many coachbuilders were to merge and names disappear or be sold on. The 1948 show was reported to be the last at which Gurney Nutting exhibited.

Moving down the 1948-limousine pecking order, there was still some patronage to be had from Daimler, still the favoured car of the Royal Family. Bodied by Barker & Co., its own coachbuilder, the Sports Special drophead coupé was also offered with a Tickford body, while the vast Daimler Straight Eight was offered with a Windover body. Daimler was set to have a turbulent decline in the 1950s with some coach-built adventures along the way.

Mass-market carmakers that produced a limousine in their catalogue entrusted the job of trimming and building them to coachbuilding firms they already owned to add a touch of snob appeal. Rootes' top-marque Humber provided the Pullman limousine, with a body built by Thrupp & Maberley. Austin, lacking a prestige name, had bought the London firm of Vanden Plas in 1946 and its first main product was the A125 Princess, almost the same car as the Austin Sheerline, apart from more swooping lines.

The coachwork section accommodated purveyors of bodywork for Rolls-Royce and Bentley plus carmakers' luxury divisions. Here, in 1951, Thrupp & Maberley show a couple of Humber Pullman limousines and a Sunbeam-Talbot convertible. (Rootes, courtesy of Coventry History Centre)

sales success, with 29,000 produced in the first year of production, with 75 per cent exported. It was first offered as a two-door saloon or convertible but a four-door, estate and van would follow and it would become somewhat of a national treasure.

Bringing up the six-seater saloon side, the Morris Oxford and Six resembled scaled-up versions of the Minor, while the Wolseley 4/50 and 6/80 were better-trimmed versions of the same cars – the company and name owned by Morris since 1927.

There was internal competition from the Riley brand, which Morris had bought in 1938. Over on stand 141, the RMA and RMB saloons were well away from Morris and distinctly different from the Oxfords, with 1.5- or 2.5-litre twin-overhead camshaft engines and rakishly British bodywork built over an ash frame. Once more with an eye to American buyers, a convertible version was launched at the show, but this was even more of a flop than Austin's Atlantic, with 507 sold up to 1950. It was the last Riley to be considered an individual design. Even before merging with Austin in 1952, Nuffield realised it had to rationalise its brands until the badges and grilles were the only things to set them apart.

The ancient Coventry marque of Singer, a thriving producer in the 1920s was struggling with a heavily bombed factory but nonetheless fronted its contribution to the export drive (no British price was listed), the new SM 1500 saloon. Technically up with its competitors in its use of independent front suspension and an overhead camshaft engine, it was sadly the plainest looking with unflattering slab-sided styling.

Vauxhall too had swept away its pre-war range in favour of a single new model for 1949 the L Series, a mid-sized saloon in miniature Chevrolet shape (as befitted Vauxhall's US owners) offered as the Wyvern with four cylinders, Velox with six.

The Rootes Group (then Hillman, Humber and Sunbeam) contributed 10.7 per cent to British car production and also dutifully produced a single model Hillman for 1949, the 1.2-litre Minx.

On the other hand the shapely Sunbeam-Talbot 80 and 90 of 1948 were considered the height of US-influenced style. Rootes had bought Sunbeam-Talbot Darracq in 1935 and applied the name to its sporting cars. The 1.2-litre 80 and 2.0-litre 90 were announced in July 1948. The cars were styled in-house, although Sir William and Reginald Rootes were early advocates of American design and had contracted the famous US industrial designer Raymond Loewy in

1938 to add his touch to its marques. He contributed the interior of the 80 and 90.

Ford had squeezed twelve cars on to an Earls Court stand equal in size to Morris's. But it fielded no 'new style' cars in 1948. The Anglia held the title of Britain's least expensive car at £309 tax paid, then came the Prefect and the large V8 Pilot from 1947, a reworked design from America but nonetheless novel, favoured by cops and robbers alike.

By contrast to these sensible saloon cars, British motorists had their first chance to see a short straight-sided vehicle called a Land Rover, sharing stand space with the Rover 60 saloon.

It's an often-recounted story but worth telling again. The Land Rover came into being because the ex-Second World War Jeep, which Rover's technical director Maurice Wilks had been using on his Anglesey farm, was due for replacement and it became apparent that there was nothing else then on sale which compared to this go-anywhere, four-wheel-drive workhorse.

Production of twenty-five pilot vehicles (later fifty) was sanctioned by the Rover board in September 1947 and the strong steel chassis was panelled in aluminium, not rationed because of its extensive use in aircraft manufacture. Initially powered by a four-cylinder 1.6-litre Rover 60 engine, drive could be transferred from rear to all four wheels by an additional transfer gearbox which gave eight ratios for tackling every kind of terrain. Stafford Cripps appreciated the potential of such a vehicle to help exports and domestic agriculture and, having been appointed Chancellor of the Exchequer in late 1947, exempted the Land Rover from purchase tax. Primarily aimed at agricultural use across the world, it was intended as a short-lived export earner. Launched at the April 1948 Amsterdam Motor Show and then the British Royal Bath and West Agricultural Show, the Land Rover had gone into production in July 1948, and by the time of Earls Court Rover had been swamped with orders. The new addition at the October show was a Land Rover estate wagon. More car-like, it was a distant relative of the Range Rover, but this one did attract purchase tax, taking the British price up to £959. Within a couple of years the Land Rover was outselling Rover saloons and would become the stuff of motoring legend.

At this very British show (imports were banned until 1953) Citroën and Renault both showed new models destined to become best sellers and available to home buyers as they were British-built.

THE AMERICAN CAR IN BRITAIN

Buick, Cadillac, Chevrolet, Chrysler, DeSoto, Dodge, Ford, Hudson, Lincoln, Mercury, Oldsmobile, Pontiac and Studebaker. This roll-call for American exhibitors at the 1948 show illustrates the American car as a well-established part of British motoring.

By the early 1920s a number of American manufacturers had followed the example of Ford's 1912 Model T assembly plant in Manchester, with General Motors building in Willesden, North London from 1925 and Chrysler assembling cars from Completely Knocked Down (CKD) kits in Kew from the 1930s. Packard and Hudson could be found on the nearby Great West Road from 1926.

Reliable and well built, American cars gave wealthy British buyers an alternative prestige choice. Right-hand drive (RHD) cars were also sourced from American-owned Canadian plants. Coming from a Dominion country of the British Commonwealth, Canadian cars qualified for a lower import tariff as they had to contain a proportion of locally made components. RHD transatlantic cars were also assembled in South Africa and Australia.

In 1935 the image of the American car in Britain had a huge boost when the Prince of Wales, King Edward, walked into Buick concessionaire Lendrum & Hartman's showroom in Mayfair and ordered a Roadmaster sedan. It was delivered in 1936 with another Roadmaster for his 'friend' Mrs Wallace Simpson. A further Buick went to the Duke and Duchess of Kent, provoking outrage from Rolls-Royce and Daimler.

American names were a steady feature of pre-1939 motor shows and returned en masse in 1948, although at first listed for 'exhibition only' along with other imports. Their vast size and gadgets were fascinating to the repressed British motorist. Show guides marvelled at exotically named equipment such as 'Prestomatic' transmission, 'Perma-quiet' valves and 'ParaFlex' rear springs. Purchase tax made them even more rarefied. In 1954, when prices were once again listed, an Oldsmobile 88 Super was £2,324 while a Jaguar Mk VII was £1,616.

In the 1950s and '60s American culture seeped into every part of British life and this was the heyday of US car sales in Britain. An American import was a must to show you'd made it, a first buy for pop stars, actors, impresarios and young members of the aristocracy. Racetracks thundered to the sound of Ford Galaxies, Falcons and Mustangs, which Ford of America aimed straight at the reigning Jaguar saloons. Off-track star drivers like Jack Sears and Jim Clark ran

American cars from their sponsors. In short, it was 'cool' to have an American car.

London's Great West Road was home to Lincoln Cars, which Ford of Britain used to import and promote US and German Fords, with many of the RHD American models being Canadian built. Falcons, Mustangs, Thunderbirds and Galaxies all came into Lincoln Cars and out to dealerships such as Simpsons of Wembley, which also prepared cars for the Motor Show. There was also a healthy used-car market supplied by vehicles from US Air Force bases.

British buyers' interest in American cars was waning by the late 1960s and was further dampened by the 1973 fuel crisis. Lincoln Cars had closed in 1967 and Ford imported small numbers of its American and Australian products through a central London office. Fewer and fewer American cars were to be seen at the Earls Court show, although American Motors continued to exhibit up until the mid 1970s and Chrysler, which took over Rootes in 1967, offered Canadian-built cars until 1969. After this point its only 'standard' imports were Australian.

In this wide shot of the 1948 show American marques are very much in evidence. The British Sunbeam-Talbots beyond the Dodge and Chrysler stand resemble shrunken versions. (Giles Chapman Picture Library)

Renault had been assembling cars for the British and colonial markets in Acton West London since 1928. In 1946 it had launched the rear-engined 4CV (for '*Quatre Chevaux Vapeur*' which translates as 'four steam horses', the basis of the French tax code) and British showgoers got their first chance to see it as the Renault 760.

Citroën, too, had assembled cars since 1926 at Slough to avoid 33.3 per cent import tax, and the Light Fifteen, to be better known as the Traction Avant, was the star of the 1948 stand, along with a display of its six-cylinder engine and front-wheel-drive transmission. With this and unitary construction it had been revolutionary when launched on the French market in 1935 and was already a best-seller. Slough-built Light Fifteens were endowed with leather seats and more dashboard instruments.

SPORTING FORTIES

That famous 1948 show marked the start of over a decade of British sports car success; some names are long gone but others thrived into the following century.

AC Cars (for Auto Carriers) had launched its 2-Litre saloon and drophead coupé in 1947, which looked quite unadventurous

compared to Alvis, hitherto makers of respectable sporting saloons pitching for the American market and hitting the newsreels with its whale-like 'super sports' car, the TB14, with a fold-flat windscreen, concealed convertible hood and headlamps, and a cocktail cabinet in the doors. The latter feature wisely did not make production and only 100 TB14s would be built.

Sydney Allard had built special cars for competition before the war with considerable success and the Allard Motor Company was founded in Clapham, South London in 1946. The car of the same name was a relatively new make, borrowing readily available British Ford V8 engines for hot-rod performance for the day. Allards became a big hit with US drivers, fitted with American V8s, and achieved considerable competition success.

Next in the list of new sports cars, Aston Martin had been producing cars since 1914 but lurched from one financial crisis to another. In 1947 it was purchased by tractor and gear manufacturer David Brown along with the Lagonda company via an advert in *The Times* which merely offered a car company for sale.

The first new post-war Aston Martin, the 2-Litre Sports (retrospectively titled the DB1) was launched at the 1948 show at a heady £2,331 with tax. Also a drophead coupé but more stately in appearance than the TB14, the Lagonda 2.6-Litre was also launched

Caravanning boomed in the 1940s and '50s. Here the Caravan Club South London travels through Brighton in 1954. Leading is a 1950 Bailey Maestro towed by a 1954 Ford Zephyr Six. (Caravan Club)

in 1948, with an advanced twin-overhead camshaft engine designed by W.O. Bentley, also available as a saloon.

German cars may have been an understandable no-go for the 1948 show but their sporting influence was present. The Bristol Aeroplane Company had entered the car market in 1946 with the Bristol 400, a coupé bearing a distinct resemblance to the pre-war Type 328 Frazer-Nash-BMW. It was part of the spoils of war. According to *Britain's Motor Industry: The First 100 Years*, during 1945 AFN, the makers of the Frazer-Nash and BMW importer had visited BMW's bombed-out works in Munich and come away with a 328 built for the 1940 Mille Miglia race and at Bristol's request made a further trip to come away with technical drawings for a number of models. The hand-built Bristol 400 was composed of a BMW chassis and engine, and BMW-inspired styling; it lasted until 1950. At the 1948 show the 400 was joined by the exceptionally aerodynamic 401 saloon and 402 convertible (even the door handles were concealed), genuine 100mph cars with a price tag of over £3,000 which ensured exclusivity.

Frazer-Nash continued to use BMW engines and running gear but they were reclothed in their own styling for 1948.

The Donald Healey Motor Company had only been established in 1945, but by 1948 its sports saloons were riding high and record-breaking. The 2.5-litre Healey Elliott had achieved a very notable 106.56mph on the Milan–Como autostrada, then beaten it with 111.87mph on the newly completed Jabbeke highway in Belgium, the fastest top speed for a closed production car, and that achieved on poor-grade pool petrol.

There being no motorways in Britain at the time, there was no straight stretch of road long enough to publicly test the claimed top speeds. After Healey, British carmakers beat a path to Jabbeke for an expedient way to set records and then glory in the publicity value. A stretch would be closed off and top speeds would be measured and certified by the Royal Automobile Club of Belgium. New for the show was the Healey 'Sportsmobile', a convertible of modern but somewhat slab-sided lines said to have been bodied by a coachbuilding firm in Slough. Just twenty-three are recorded as having been made in 1948.

But there was an out-and-out sports car star of the 1948 show, the Jaguar Speedster or Super Sports, soon renamed the XK120, after the new range of engines it ushered in and its top speed. The former

Swallow Sidecar Company of Coventry had dropped the SS name in favour of Jaguar.

September had seen the introduction of the Mk V Jaguar saloon and the Speedster was based on a shortened version of its chassis but powered by a new engine design, the XK Series, which would power all Jaguars for decades. In that sense the sports car was seen by founder Sir William Lyons as a small volume testbed and publicity generator for the saloon car engines Jaguar had developed during the war. The first production XK engine was an in-line 3442cc twin-overhead camshaft design producing a remarkable 160bhp. The streamlined styling was influenced by the same special BMW 328 which had done the rounds of British carmakers – Jaguar as well as Bristol.

'At any price these "XK" Jaguar super sports would be remarkable cars, but with their basic price in this country set at £988, their world-wide success is assured,' *Motor Sport* magazine would write in 1949. 'Motor Sport is receiving inquiries about them from America, Kenya and other places overseas, and we understand that already enthusiasts in the States are building up a substantial waiting-list.' Before it was replaced by the XK140 in 1955, 9 per cent of XK120s were exported.

Jaguar's claim of a 120mph top speed aroused some scepticism so it had to head to Jabekke in 1949 as Healey had done, where a standard XK120 achieved 126mph and 132.5mph with the windscreen removed. In 1953 Jaguar test driver Norman Dewis set a new production car speed record at an average speed of 172.4mph in a highly streamlined version.

MG was slower to modernise its cars after 1945 but that proved little handicap to sales. The 1948 MG TC two-seater sports car on the stand was far from the latest thing, being a 1945 version of the pre-war TB. It was short-lived with a production run of 10,000 but laid the foundations for MG's huge success in America the following decade. American soldiers stationed in the UK during the war had picked up a taste for nimble British roadsters. The newer offering on the MG stand was a four-door convertible based on the Y saloon 'which has been requested from overseas'. Not that strong a request, as it turned out, with 877 sold to 1950.

By the time the first post-war British International Motor Show closed it had clocked up a record attendance of 562,000. Nearly 97,000 people had squeezed in on Saturday 30 October alone.

FALTERING ATTENTION

The 1949 show nearly didn't happen, as 2,000 strikers at Earls Court and Olympia threatened to derail the start. After thirty-six hours of talks, the dispute was only resolved moments before the show opened.

The British motorist was still beset with restrictions on the purchase and use of cars. The standard ration of fuel had only slightly increased to the equivalent of 6 miles a day for three months in the summer and was back to 90 miles, or around 3 miles a day, by show time. Just 60,000 cars were allocated to the home market and 24,590 cars and chassis were exported in September 1949 alone.

With such a burst of new models at the 1948 show, the 1949 event was one of consolidation for most manufacturers. The most startling 1949 debut was the Rover 75. Renowned for its conservative designs, Rover caused consternation with this slab-sided saloon without the separate wings that had characterised the pre-war car. Most controversial was a single central fog light – nicknamed the 'Cyclops' eye' – in the middle of what should have been a traditional Rover radiator grille. The overall proportions were heavily influenced by the Raymond Loewy-styled Studebaker Commander, an example of which had been used by Rover in developing its new car – known internally as the P4. The third eye was short-lived, being replaced by a simpler grille in 1952, and the developed range enjoyed a distinguished career to 1964.

Triumph unsuccessfully transferred the mini-Rolls-Royce looks of its 1800 saloon to the smaller Mayflower – referred to as 'razor edge' styling – for a small upright car with a stately body which looked like it was going to topple off its own wheels. It was aimed at the American market with a name recalling the ship of the Pilgrim Fathers but did not settle. It was not a complete dud, though, with 35,000 made between 1950 and 1953, joined by a small run of convertibles. The 1800 became the Renown with the fitting of the 2.1-litre Standard Vanguard engine.

With there being little chance of British buyers getting a new car, there proved to be a striking drop in attendance, down by some 200,000 to 355,486 according to the post-show bulletin from the SMMT. It trumpeted that interest from overseas buyers was even greater in 1949 and *The Autocar* positively added that with less of a crush around the stands it was easier to do business (with the people who actually had money). 'Export or die' was working in the short term and Britain was the world's leading exporter of cars in 1949; a position it held until displaced by Germany in 1956. Reportedly some 8,000 honoured foreigners with money in their pockets had been specially invited and some were no doubt wined and dined in their own lounge on the second floor behind the Warwick Road entrance. Good times for British motorists seemed far off as the 1950s beckoned.

The 1949 Rover 75 suddenly brought the company bang up to date and the following year formed the basis of the world's first gas turbine car. (Newspress)

There were always two motor shows at Earls Court: the one put on for press only on the preview day and the one that opened to the public the day after.

Then, as now, press day was about catching the camera's eye, not least British Pathé news, which until the 1960s was still chronicling modern life for cinema newsreels when TV ownership was not widespread. Celebrities would mill around, occasionally bringing it to a halt as Peter Sellers and The Beatles did in the 1960s. In the 1970s naked women caused the greatest need for crowd control.

On the second-floor mezzanine a large press room was filled with the sound of many correspondents bashing typewriters, a press cuttings service, lines of telephones and a scoreboard keeping account of attendance figures. Staff from the Society of Motor Manufacturers (SMMT) were always on hand.

But while some journalists were busy generating copy, for many the afternoon of press day was an alcohol-fuelled washout, due in no small part to the British Motor Corporation (BMC) lunch which drew in hundreds of hungry hacks.

The overseas journalists were as welcomed as the buyers (and British writers could expect the same when they went to Paris or Geneva). In 1944 two notable British motoring journalists, Laurie Cade and Dudley Noble, formed the Motoring Correspondents' Circle, a dining club at which industry figures were invited to speak. This became the Guild of Motoring Writers, in 1946, representing the wider interests of the profession. The first Guild Motor Show test day was held at the newly created Goodwood race circuit in 1949 for British scribes and the industry to show off the latest machinery to the foreign press.

The importance of press day was eventually devalued. By the 1970s you could wrangle your way into Earls Court to ogle the ladies, grab brochures and have drinks without being a journalist if you had connections. Gordon Wilkins in the 1976 *Daily Express Guide to 1977 Cars* longed for the old days: 'Press day 1937 at the time was just for press and not for the hordes of friends and the nude models who in recent years hid the cars, filled the front pages, and then got dressed and went home before the public arrived.'

Some people *were* working though. If you were going to buy one car magazine that year, you bought the show guide. Britain's

then two competing motoring weeklies (they merged in 1988) *The Autocar* and *Motor* would produce a bumper edition with a guide to the show and all the cars by stand on sale at 10 a.m. on opening day. 'The annual *Autocar* Motor Show issues were a "must" for every petrolhead pre-1990,' Recalls Geoff Howard, who joined the magazine in 1962:

I think we sold over 200,000 copies most years, compared to around 100,000 as the regular circulation. So by the time Earls Court opened we had done most of our work – going to the show was a welcome break from all the late nights in the weeks before. There were interviews with industry people at the show, but mainly it was time to party on the stands, where the hospitality was always generous, and outside in the bars and restaurants of South Ken., Chelsea and the West End.

Press facilities at Earls Court 1955 consisted of coat racks and tables with press releases. The man on the right is viewing slides at a Rootes 'literature dispenser'. (Rootes, courtesy of Coventry History Centre)

3 AUSTERITY TO INNOVATION 1950–59

The dawn of a new decade seldom seems much different from the previous year and 1950 still offered gloomy prospects for British new-car buyers as the number of home market cars had to be further reduced. However, Britain was the world's leading exporter of cars in 1950 with 398,300 leaving its shores. And petrol rationing ended.

The first show of the decade was opened by a full quota of royalty: King George VI and the Queen, accompanied by Princess Elizabeth and the Duke of Edinburgh. Overseas visitors were still treated like royalty with their own lounge staffed by members of the SMMT overseas department, with interpreters on hand.

From the 1940s to the '60s the opening day of the show was marked by manufacturers announcing how many export orders they had generated. 'You knew how many cars you were going to build in the next six months so you just multiplied them by a domestic number,' recalls Harry Calton, who joined Ford of England in 1952 as a junior clerk in the Public Relations Department (the start of a long career):

Then in the second week, later in the life of the show, you had orders from fleet owners. Part of their deal was that they liked to be seen on the stand and they were photographed shaking hands with either the chairman or the managing director with the fleet manager in the background.

Having seen all its rivals produce new models since 1945, the first all-new Ford of England design broke cover. The 1950 four-cylinder Consul and six-cylinder Zephyr saloons marked a number of firsts for the company. Bodywork was of monocoque construction and the Consul's four-cylinder, 1508cc, 47bhp engine was Ford of Britain's first overhead valve unit of oversquare dimensions, meaning that its cylinders had a greater bore diameter than its stroke length, enabling better performance through bigger valves and improving engine wear. The Zephyr featured a 2.2-litre six-cylinder engine of 68bhp.

Jowett, the little carmaker from Bradford was still riding high on the success of the Javelin saloon and had taken on extra factory space. At the 1949 show it had created a stir with a prototype chassis for a sports car and the following spring the Jupiter had been announced with a hand-built body on a tubular spaceframe chassis constructed by a German former Auto Union designer. Good for 90mph, a Jupiter triumphed in its class at Le Mans that year.

Having failed to set pulses racing in America, Austin's A90 Atlantic was followed by the A40 sports, a 1200cc convertible based on the larger Jensen Interceptor body. The Jensen Interceptor was also new in 1950 and was the company's first sports car.

Jaguar, riding a wave of success from the XK120, introduced the Mk VII saloon (there was no Mk VI as Bentley was using that title), with the same 3.5-litre engine giving a claimed 100mph performance. It almost lived up to Jaguar's long-lived slogan, 'Grace … Space … Pace', at 16ft long and at nearly 2 tons it only managed 16mpg: little matter for the US market it was aimed at.

Aston Martin was also entering the 1950s with acclaim, and the British public had its first chance to get close to the new DB2 coupé and convertible. Owner David Brown had embarked on an ambitious racing programme with the prototype DB2 and it had paid off with two cars making fifth, and six overall places at the 1950 24 Hours of Le Mans endurance race. Success really counted in sales terms. A road-going DB2 was launched in April 1950, replacing the 2-litre Sports with the Lagonda's advanced six-cylinder 2-litre engine giving 105bhp.

While the DB2 fixed-head coupé was £1,914, sports car fans with smaller pockets could have an MG TD Midget for £470 basic on stand 154, although again much of MG's output was destined for America. It had the traditional pre-war lines but new independent front suspension.

1951

Britain had something tangible to cheer itself up with in 1951: the Festival of Britain, a countrywide celebration of old and new, including cars. The focus was on a specially constructed exhibition site on London's South Bank, which reportedly took in 8.5 million visitors over five months until it closed in September 1951. It risked making the Earls Court exhibition centre look somewhat old hat.

Two thousand overseas buyers were said to have attended the 1950 Motor Show but *The Autocar* predicted the numbers of domestic visitors, not willing to stand another year of window-shopping for cars they couldn't buy or couldn't afford, would fall. One reader wrote that they had recently cancelled an order for a car, placed in 1947, and were having trouble getting the £5 deposit back.

The star of the 1951 show was small, cheap and stood on a turntable of quilted crimson velvet. Until then new small British car designs had been neglected in favour of large-engine export models aside from the Morris Minor, so the Austin A30 or 'New Seven' was big news. Back at Austin's Longbridge factory in Birmingham a crowd of 20,000 reportedly queued to see it. At £504 with tax, it just undercut the £530 Morris Minor.

At just over 11ft long, it was regarded as a smart piece of styling which stood apart from its American-influenced brethren. The 'New Seven' title was intended to evoke the much-loved people's car of

The 1951 Austin A30 has the stand built around it. Some carmakers are more ready than others. Sometimes on press day there was a big hole where a car arrived late for dramatic effect. (Mirrorpix)

Caught by *The Autocar*'s camera in 1951, this man was probably being told that he could be waiting years for his new car. (LAT)

A lady (one assumes of certain means) is more interested in the news than the new Aston Martin DB2. (LAT)

the 1920s, but it was right up to date: Austin's first car with unitary construction, produced from early 1952 initially as a four-door then a two. Its electrical system was 12 volt when many cars were still 6, and its new 30bhp four-cylinder 803cc engine, the A Series, was soon enlarged and would propel generations of future BMC cars including the Mini, and only end production, after much development, in 2000. The A30 became the A35 in 1956 with a 948cc engine.

In a year where there were few totally new designs Vauxhall's new Velox and Wyverns gave the baby Austin some competition. The Luton manufacturer's styling was, as ever, influenced by parent company General Motors, in this case a 1949 Chevrolet. Competitors to the Ford Consul and Zephyr, the Wyvern was given four cylinders; the Velox six. A small idea ahead of its time was an interior release for the boot lid. They were offered in such jolly paint colours as Caribbean blue, cloud-mist grey, forest green and sand beige.

Ferrari made its first appearance at a London Motor Show courtesy of Brooklands of Bond Street, showing a long wheelbase 212 Export, a 212 chassis and a Type 342 America four-seat coupé with bodywork by Turin coachbuilder Ghia. Created in 1947, Ferrari was

relatively new to producing road cars and the 212, like others, would be bodied by different Italian coachbuilders such as Ghia, Touring or Vignale. The 212's V12 2.6-litre 140bhp engine and five-speed gearbox were astonishing to British motorists; the 220bhp of the 4.1-litre Type 342 America even more so.

And 1951 was the first year of a series of 'Docker Daimlers' built for the company director's wife, Lady Norah Docker, by Hooper. Depending on your viewpoint, they stood for outright glamour or outright gaudiness. Starting with the 'Gold Car', they deserve their own story (see p.40). The second most distinctive coach-built car was Harold Radford's Bentley Mk VI Countryman, an upper-class estate car conversion with a split tailgate, folding rear seats and optional extras including electric rear seats and an electric razor. Tax paid, it was an awesome £6,604.

Given a small footnote of press coverage, a couple of Porsches marked the re-appearance of a German car at Earls Court, although not on a manufacturer stand but displayed by Connaught Engineering. The performance squeezed from their 1086cc engines was considered remarkable.

CAR RADIO

If you couldn't buy the cars downstairs at the early 1950s Earls Court shows, you could part with cash upstairs at the trade and accessory stands, or at least get some inspiration.

For many years the ultimate accessory was a car radio and at first the most expensive. In 1948 a radio was, on average, £30 with tax, equating to a surprising £1,047 in inflation-adjusted modern-day money. Only American cars and limousines came with standard radios and cheaper new cars were only just beginning to allow space in the dashboard for control units.

Radio had helped the nation through the war and there was a great appetite for 'company in the car' rather than 'in-car entertainment'. The BBC only offered the Home Service and the Light Programme, and Radio Luxemburg, launched in 1948, was the only station playing popular music.

Each September Earls Court played host to the Radio Show. Firms such as Philips, EKCO and Motorola worked flat out producing radiograms for home and export use, in large cabinets. They all contained a number of 'valves', which, in simple terms, were glass tubes containing a vacuum with a metal filament inside them, called thermionic valves. When current was passed through them they amplified radio signals. These valves needed space and 220 volts, which made car-sized packages difficult. Car radios could be bulky all-in-one units but were often split into the controls, single speaker and a further box with the electrical parts, including a 'vibrator' to step up the 1940s cars' 6- or 12-volt current to around 200 volts DC and heat the valves to their operating temperature. Suppressors had to be fitted on the ignition system to stop it interfering with the sound.

The author's father, Ray Hayes, was a radio and television engineer between the 1940s and '60s, and fitted many early car radios. 'They were supplied with brackets to fit under the dashboard or wherever it would go. If the set was split, the power pack had to go under the bonnet. There were all sorts of combinations,' he recalls. 'It could take me up to half a day including fitting an aerial and routing the wiring.'

From the mid 1950s, transistors replaced valves, dramatically shrinking home and car equipment and giving us the first portable radios. Sales could be measured by the amount of car radio licences in force, rising from 99,579 in 1951 to 445,258 in 1960. A car transistor required no extra licence if you already had a home set.

Take the **tedium** out of travel!

Long journeys are far less tedious when your car is fitted with Ekco Car Radio. The latest Ekco model CR117 can be easily installed in cars of any make or year, either as a single unit or as three separate units — Power Pack, Receiver, and Speaker. Magnetic Core Self-Set Tuning enables you to use any of the 3 pre-set stations without cancelling the one last tuned by hand. Pressure on the appropriate wavelength button returns you automatically to the station last selected by manual tuning. **£30** tax paid.

MODEL CR117 — 6-valve, quality built superhet, press-button control and manual tuning on Long and Medium waves. R.F. stage for increased sensitivity. Magnifying Diakon tuning scale with variable dimming switch. Three-position tone control for 6 or 12-volt operation at low battery drain. In Black with Green scale or Beige with Maroon scale.

EKCO CAR RADIO

E. K. COLE LTD., SOUTHEND-ON-SEA, ESSEX

If you had no hope of securing a new car, the top accessory for your old banger was a radio, highly prized and highly priced in 1951. (Author's collection)

1952

By the time the 1952 show opened its doors there was a new Conservative government, with a surprise return by Winston Churchill, and the British motor industry had undergone a change that would lead to the downfall of famous names decades later.

A merger between Austin and Morris had been debated for many years (delayed by the strong wills of Lord Nuffield and Leonard Lord) but after protracted negotiations the British Motor Corporation (BMC) was created in February 1952.

From its very early days the BMC range of cars was vast. The badges spanned Austin, Morris, MG, Austin-Healey, Riley and Wolseley. Starting with the baby Austin A30 then the slightly bigger Morris Minor, there was a steady progression through family saloons to the six-cylinder cars, such as the Oxford MO and Wolseley 4/44. MG and later Austin-Healey mopped up sports cars and Vanden Plas provided the range-topping Princess. This was aside from a large commercial vehicles division. While a certain rationalisation of engines took place as the company was formed, post-merger BMC's 'badge engineering' accelerated.

The year of 1952 was the start of a golden age for affordable British sports cars. Everybody wanted a slice of that dollar market and was still chasing North American buyers into the 1950s, especially sports car sales. Even with its pre-war looks the MG TD was cleaning up 'Stateside' (by 1952 the best-selling import) and now Triumph and Austin announced serious competition.

Flushed with the success of the Vanguard, Sir John Black of Standard Triumph had been determined to bring a credible Triumph sports car to market after the sedate Triumph Roadster proved no match to the Jaguar XK 120. Walter Belgrove's costly aerodynamic TR-X was shown at the 1950 Paris Motor Show but never produced.

So the white Triumph 20 TS (retrospectively named TR1) was a show surprise. This was a basic sports car with cut down doors and a Standard Vanguard-derived 1991cc engine tuned for 90bhp. It seemed a performance bargain with a pre-tax price of £555 but its rushed development showed in very poor handling. A chassis redesign and a longer rear end to give better luggage space resulted in the TR2 launched at the 1953 Geneva Motor Show. This was the true start of a TR line that culminated in the wedge-shaped Triumph TR7 of 1975.

Having failed to attract the sportier American buyer with the 1948 Atlantic and the A40 Sports, Austin scored a direct hit in 1952 with the Austin-Healey 100. Its conception and naming has been the subject of a little Earls Court myth-making.

Donald Healey's Motor Company had continued producing well-respected but expensive sporting cars based on Riley engines. Trying to keep his company afloat, he formed an alliance with the Nash-Kelvinator Corporation to design and initially assemble the export-only Nash-Healey between 1950 and 1954, billed as America's first post-war sports car.

Healey, though, saw the future of his company as dependent on a cheaper-to-build sports car using as many Austin components as possible and therefore developed the Healey Hundred from 1951 with a great deal of Austin A90 components, including its 2660cc four-cylinder engine producing, like the Triumph, 90bhp.

The story goes that the Healey Hundred started the beginning of the 1952 Earls Court show as a Healey but by the end had become an Austin-Healey after Leonard Lord of Austin/BMC, seeing the prototype on press day, signed a deal to create the first Austin-Healey. Donald Healey was retained as a consultant and the car was assembled in Austin's own Longbridge factory, not Warwick.

Healey authority Jon Pressnell unpicks the tale in *Austin-Healey: The Bulldog Breed*. While the very public signing suggested a spontaneous decision, the British motor industry was close-knit enough that an A90-based Healey sports car was known about at Austin before October 1952. Just before the show Healey had given famous *Autosport* writer John Bolster a prototype in which he achieved 106mph at Jabekke. There was not, as has been recounted, a 'contest' between other sports car makers for the contract and the deal had been drawn up on paper before the theatrical handshake occurred.

Britain was enjoying a surge of motor racing, especially amateur motor sport on former Second World War aerodromes. By 1952 the country had three official racing circuits: former bomber training base Silverstone, Brands Hatch and Goodwood.

Racing cars were admitted to the show for the first time, with a stand comprising a Formula 2 Cooper Bristol, Hersham and Walter Motors (HWM), Alta, a Connaught and a Frazer-Nash. Record-breaking production cars, rally and touring cars were always allowed, but the SMMT's attitude to racing cars on the ground floor was a bit schizophrenic. They were banished in 1954 and such was the resentment over the non-appearance of a victorious Vanwall in 1958 that the British Racing & Sports Car Club (BRSCC) came up with the Racing Car Show, amply filled with everything from Grand Prix cars to tuning parts and accessories, in January 1960. It found an instant audience and became an annual tradition, long outlasting the Motor Show.

On the 1952 luxury saloon car side, Coventry carmaker Armstrong Siddeley aimed hopefully at Jaguar with its stately new 3.4-litre Sapphire saloon. As part of the Hawker Siddeley Group its adverts boasted that this was 'The pedigree car with the jet-bred engine', built on the same production line as the Sapphire jet. A daring and complex feature was a four-speed pre-selector gearbox, with electric and push-button control, called 'Selectric'.

Not having given Bentley much attention in the post-war years, in 1952 Rolls-Royce ensured it made its mark in automotive history with the beautiful fastback Continental R, bodied by H.J. Mulliner & Co. It was a £4,890 car in which the super-rich could cruise down to the South of France at over 100mph in supreme comfort and became the styling inspiration behind the brand's rebirth under BMW decades later.

A fine array of 1953 models, including an Austin-Healey 100 (front middle), is readied for the overseas press at the Guild of Motoring Writers' test day at Goodwood. (Guild of Motoring Writers)

1953

The supply of new cars for the home market finally began to ease up during 1953, with fewer being subject to the covenant. The motoring public clearly responded; Earls Court historian John Glanfield recounts that the 1953 Motor Show drew such a crowd on its first day (21 October) that queues ran a mile long and ten deep and blocked the traffic. The police ordered the show open early, and by 11 a.m. 130,310 visitors were reported to have been admitted. Final attendance was a record 612,953. You could only fully see cars on the stands from the gallery.

Although expensive cars were enclosed and viewed by invitation, and star cars were on plinths or turntables, the rest were left on the floor at the mercy of the public, some of whom were tempted to take home a souvenir or a spare part. Gear knobs were fair game and Ford's Harry Calton recalls a front seat of a Popular vanishing by about 3 p.m. In any case, front seats often had to be changed mid-show through simple wear and tear, and if a door was scratched, then a small team would replace it overnight.

This year it was Ford's turn in the small-car limelight with the new Anglia 100E (Ford of Britain's model names at the time had

The dazzling Bentley Continental R coupé sits behind a Mk VI saloon at the 1953 show. On the stand beyond, the Armstrong-Siddeley Sapphire was new but the company slowly declined during the decade. (Bentley)

an E for England) Anglia and Prefect family. Designed and styled in England rather than Detroit, they resembled a scaled-down Consul. The basic Anglia came with two doors, the Prefect with four, once more featuring MacPherson strut suspension, but, at a time when an overhead valve engine was becoming the norm, they appeared technologically backward with sidevalve engines of the same 1172cc capacity as the elderly outgoing model. It was, in fact, an all-new unit but one that used a familiar capacity to allow existing production machinery to be carried over, saving funds that had been expended during the development of the Consul.

The British small car had definitely returned. Standard Triumph completed its range with the little Standard Eight, named after a pre-war model: yours for a mere £339 basic (£481 total) compared to the £355 Austin A30 and the £360 Anglia.

Compared to the Eight, the Austin A30's specification looked luxurious. The new baby Standard did have four doors but its exterior lacked any embellishment beyond bumpers (hubcaps were extra) with a mesh-backed recess instead of a radiator grille. There was no boot lid. Access to this space was via split folding rear seat backs – decades before hatchbacks came with the same feature. The spare wheel, on the other hand, could be accessed from outside from a panel behind the number plate.

The Eight's engine was an all-new 803cc four-cylinder overhead valve unit. Developed and enlarged versions were destined to power small Triumph saloons and sports cars well into the 1970s.

The Standard's minimalism was nothing compared to the first appearance of the Citroën 2CV at a British motor show and due to be assembled at Slough in 1954 for British and export markets. A project started in 1936 but curtailed by war, the 2CV had been unveiled at the 1948 Paris Motor Show and went into production the following year. With a canvas roof, hammock seats and a tail-up stance due to its unique long-travel suspension, the 2CV looked like nothing on Earth. Its two-cylinder air-cooled engine of 375cc gave a top speed of 40.9mph when tested by *Motor,* and 54.7mpg even when driven hard. At first it was ridiculed, but then in France waiting lists built up and it became a national treasure. In England it was sold as a saloon, light van and pick-up, but sales were hampered by its weirdness and price: £565 with tax when an Austin A30 was £476.

Funny French cars were all very well, but in 1953 the Germans returned, with Mercedes-Benz, Borgward, BMW and Volkswagen on show. Disgusted readers would write to car magazines if they showed too much enthusiasm for German products and call them pro-Nazi.

The German cars were technically fascinating. The Mercedes 170SD and the Borgward Hansa 1800 saloons both had diesel engines when British firms only fitted them to commercial vehicles. The Volkswagen Beetle, said *Motorsport*, was 'a car bound to appeal to engineers. It also represents a very pleasant form of semi-sports saloon for four persons, freeze-proof in winter, adequately fan-cooled in summer, which gives the excellent fuel consumption of at least 36mpg.'

On the sports car side, AC Cars of Thames Ditton drew admiring looks for its new ACE sports car, an alloy-bodied creation that resembled a small Ferrari. Its spaceframe chassis and all-independent suspension followed racing practice but at first the familiar 85bhp 2-litre engine was underwhelming. The little Ace was to get ever-larger engines until it became the mighty Cobra in the 1960s.

Somewhat overshadowed by its Austin-Healey stablemate in the BMC range, MG was sticking to the pre-war looks formula (having sold 25,000 Midgets in America since 1946) in the shape of the TF with a sloping radiator and a beefed up 1250cc engine, which grew to 1500cc the following year, the last gasp of the traditional MG.

The Morgan Motor Company of Malvern in Worcestershire, founded in 1910, had felt no need to update the pre-war looks of its hand-built sports cars and a sufficient amount of customers, especially stateside, were happy that its cars were stuck in a styling time warp, changing in detail year on year and when supplies of whoever's engine they were using – Standard, Triumph and Ford in the 1950s – dried up.

Having launched its moderately successful Conquest saloon in 1953, Daimler made an ill-fated entry into the two-seater market with the Conquest Roadster. Its 2.4-litre engine gave it 100bhp for 100mph but an Austin-Healey 100 cost less and looked a lot better.

Jowett showed its R4 Le Mans replica version of the Jupiter but the company was in real trouble. It had racked up debts in its rapid expansion then been hit by a slump in sales. In 1953 Ford of Britain swallowed up Briggs, which had carried out work for Austin, Rootes and Standard, as well as building bodies for Lanchester and Jowett. In September 1953 Jowett glumly announced the end of the Javelin as it could no longer rely on a supply of bodies (the Jupiter's panels were made in-house), but the problems had been more of its own making, and it ceased to be in 1954.

THE DOCKER DAIMLERS

Gold-plated fittings and zebra-skin seats were the last things one expected from stuffy old Daimler, but between 1951 and 1955 the Docker Daimlers' were an annual Earls Court spectacle.

Supplier of cars to the British monarchy since 1902, in the early 1950s Daimler was enjoying the patronage of seven royal families around the world, according to automotive historian Jonathan Wood. However, showing a sign that its grip was slipping, future queen, Princess Elizabeth, had ordered a Rolls-Royce Phantom IV in 1950.

Booming motorcycle sales from its parent, the Birmingham Small Arms (BSA), disguised loss-making cars. Daimler's post-war product range grew to ten strong by 1955 when everyone else was cutting down. Its designs seemed dated and Jaguar undercut them with its new sports saloons. Enter Sir Bernard and Lady Norah Docker. Sir Bernard had taken over from his father as managing director in 1944 and in 1949 was somewhat taken over by his marriage to the formidable Norah Royce Turner, a former dancer at the Café de Paris who already had two marriages to wealthy businessmen behind her. Norah sought to cheer the poor up. 'We bring glamour and happiness into drab lives,' she said, and carried on spending. Daimler had taken over the coachbuilder Hooper in 1940 and Sir Bernard made Norah a director and installed a drawing board in their Mayfair home.

The 1951 Gold Car was based on the Straight Eight Hooper touring limousine, finished in black with 7,000 gold stars on its side. Every piece of bright metal on the exterior was gold plated, even to the bumpers, wheel discs and radiator shell, and many interior fittings were made of solid gold. It was the last thing people expected from Daimler. Reactions were split, but in its 1951 show critique *The Autocar* bemoaned the inherent conservatism of Britain's coachbuilders and heaped praise on Bernard rather than Norah: 'It is a magnificent gesture of defiance against the doctrine that all men should be satisfied with such amenities as the State cares to hand out with the rations.'

With each year the cost and splendour of the Docker Daimlers increased. In 1954 the extravagance was Stardust, built at a reported cost of £12,500, finished in royal blue and silver with 5,000 six-pointed stars on the outside and a bonnet mascot dancer modelled on the lady herself. The rear compartment was finished in silver grey silk and blue crocodile skin trim. The animal world paid

the price for the Docker Daimlers – the 1955 Ivory White Golden Zebra was upholstered in zebra, 'Because Mink is too hot to sit on.'

In 1956 the Dockers shipped the last two cars to Monaco, where they had been invited to the wedding of Prince Rainier and Grace Kelly, at a reported cost to Daimler of £2,140. The board, realising that this was more for the couple's amusement than Daimler's sales, could finally take no more when Sir Bernard shoehorned his brother-in-law into a BSA directorship. On 30 May 1956, in full glare of the cameras, Sir Bernard was ousted and left with a £70,000 bill. The cars were stripped of their fittings and sold. The Dockers ended up living in a bungalow on Jersey. Lady Docker died in 1983 having spent her final years in the Great Western Hotel by Paddington Station.

Daimler directors Sir Bernard and Lady Norah Docker beside 1953's Silver Flash – the third in a line of show cars by Hooper. The interior was finished in black leather and red crocodile. Norah's handbags often matched. (Mirrorpix)

1954

The 1954 show was opened on 10 October by war hero Field Marshal Viscount Montgomery. *The Autocar* carried one page of new-car prices again in its regular issue. Butter, meat and cheese came off ration. Things were looking up.

The dream car of the show was undoubtedly the mighty Mercedes 300SL sports car, a supercar long before the term existed. Built to win road races and thunder down autobahns, with an advanced tubular spaceframe chassis, deep sills and imposing 'gullwing' doors, it could be calmly driven around town or reach 140mph. For £4,392 tax paid

you could have had an Aston Martin and change for an MG Midget, yet this price hardly made Mercedes-Benz a profit. Only 1,400 were built to 1957. Also new from Germany, the Borgward Isabella 1500 was admired but outpriced similar-sized British cars at £1,123.

A more affordable foreign car, built in Britain, the smart new Renault Dauphine was a successful update on the rear-engine 4CV theme.

Although they put on a brave face for the show, the fortunes of smaller Coventry carmakers Singer and Lanchester were in terminal decline. The Singer Hunter, new at the 1954 show, attempted to improve the appearance of the plain SM saloon with a new grille as

Overseas visitors received red carpet treatment during 'export or die'. Here, in 1954, a delegation from the Nigerian Marketing Board are escorted by Mr Mackie of the SMMT and his wife. (Rootes, courtesy of Coventry History Centre)

This was the reality of the jam-packed 1954 show if you weren't an overseas buyer. Britain's cheapest car, the Ford Popular, is mobbed. (Ford Motor Company Ltd)

Although the first Allards used mighty V8 engines, this 1954 Palm Beach had a range of tamer options. Behind it is the never changing shape of Morgan and, to the right, Simca. (Giles Chapman Picture Library)

the Hunter, but aroused little interest. At the end of 1955 Singer was swallowed by the Rootes Group, and its name applied to upmarket Hillmans thereafter.

Lanchester, an ancient name of British motoring, had been under the control of BSA, which in turn owned Daimler, since 1931, and the Lanchester Sprite saloon was derived from the Daimler Conquest. Just ten pre-production cars are said to have been made before the name disappeared in 1956.

1955

Something from outer space seemed to have landed on stand 155 at the 40th London Motor Show in 1955. The Citroën DS19 had no reference to past or any current car styling. Replacing the pre-war Light Fifteen, it was as if the new car hadn't just evolved but leapt several decades ahead. You could argue that no carmaker has ever been as bold since.

It drew crowds even on the British press preview day, as it had done the month before at the Paris Salon de l'Automobile. In French pronunciation, DS sounds like the word '*Déesse*', meaning goddess. Sensation doesn't quite convey the impact this car had on the automobile world.

Plenty of histories give more detail, but suffice to say it was the overall package of the DS19 which was so astonishing, especially in its most complex initial specification. Space-age styling placed red lamps in the tips of the rear pillars, mostly enclosed the rear wheels and incorporated a plastic roof. Hydraulic fluid from high-pressure pumps provided self-levelling suspension (which could run the car even on three wheels), assistance for the brakes – discs at the front – clutch actuation and steering assistance.

Displayed with no cutaways or gimmicks, the show car spoke for itself at Earls Court, merely illuminated with its doors open. Plenty of showgoers were eager to see under the bonnets of cars as they did their own maintenance, but a look under the DS bonnet, with its mass of hydraulic pipes and suspension spheres, would have sent them reeling back into Warwick Road. It was a brave purchase at £1,496 in 1955. British DS assembly at Slough started a year later, but slowed while British staff trained themselves to cope with it and because 51 per cent of components had to be

The Sunbeam Rapier was Rootes' glamour car of 1955, the 40th anniversary show. The Rapier cornered a market of its own, and proved a tough rally car. (Rootes, courtesy of Coventry History Centre)

The Citroën DS had been launched at the Paris Motor Show on 6 October 1955. It gained 750 sales in forty-five minutes: 12,000 in just one day. British buyers were more cautious. (Citroën)

British-sourced for it to escape import taxes. These included a Lucas electrical system, Connolly leather seats and incongruous wooden dashboards.

Jaguar, following victory with the D-Type at the 1955 24 Hours of Le Mans race (it would also triumph in '56 and '57) launched what would become its best-selling 2.4-litre saloon, the Mk I, for 1956 – its first unitary construction car and a bargain at £1,343. Its engine was upgraded in 1957 to 3.4 litres, losing the rear-wheel spats to become a highly successful sports saloon on road and track, and ended its career at 3.8 litres in 1968.

Grumbling from enthusiasts that MG was still stuck in the 1930s was swept aside by the new MGA, MG's first truly modern post-war sports car. The MGA was a smart, streamlined two-seater with a separate chassis but rack-and-pinion steering, independent front suspension and an Austin engine for the first time rather than Morris. The 1489cc B Series unit, tuned for 72bhp, sat naturally in performance and price below the Austin-Healey 100. With 80 per cent going to America, it lasted in various forms until 1962 and around 100,000 were built.

There was a new Austin Cambridge with unitary construction and 1200 or 1500cc engines, while the six-cylinder Austin Westminster was aimed at the flashier market occupied by the Ford Zodiac and Vauxhall Cresta with lively two-tone paint choices. Although there is little colour imagery of motor shows until the 1960s, be assured they were Technicolor experiences for visitors. 'We lived in a world without much colour,' recalls Geoff Howard, who first visited a motor show in 1955 and joined the staff of The Autocar in 1962. 'My father's cars up to 1955 had all been black (as were my first five cars from 1955 to 1960). Newspapers and even magazines like Picture Post were black and white inside, movies were very rarely in colour and post-war austerity clothing was mostly grey.'

Also invariably two-tone, Rootes showed the new Sunbeam Rapier, a smart two-door based on the new Hillman Minx with an American-style hardtop which had no central pillar so you could roll front and rear windows down for breezing down an imaginary freeway, elbow-out. The Rapier created its own market for a smart, capacious coupé and carved out a respectable career as a rally car, lasting though five generations to 1967.

The 1955 show marked a genteel revolution for Britain's finest automobile. The Rolls-Royce Silver Cloud was the first Rolls for all markets to have a unitary-construction steel body, supplied by Pressed Steel (the Bentley S1 was essentially the same car with a different bonnet and radiator). The existing six-cylinder 4887cc engine was modified for more power – although Rolls would never be so vulgar as to say what that actually was. With an eye to the all-important US market, automatic transmission derived from a GM unit was standard. Despite the majority of Clouds featuring the standard body shell, coachbuilders Park Ward, Freestone & Webb and James Young still offered individual interpretations.

A Swiss coachbuilder, Graber, provided a body style which enlivened the last days of the Alvis marque, which had been quietly sinking with ponderous saloons and bizarre-looking convertibles. It had exhibited an elegant coupé on a TC21 chassis at the 1955 Paris show and it provided the interest at Earls Court. The reception was such that Alvis made the design under licence and it evolved in closed and convertible forms until the Alvis name ceased to be applied to cars in 1967.

1956

Just as it had perked up, by autumn 1956 British motoring was about to be plunged into crisis. In July, Egyptian president, Colonel Nasser, nationalised the Suez Canal – linking the Mediterranean Sea to the Red Sea – to fund the construction of the Aswan Dam. It sent shareholders in Britain and France into shock, as the canal was a key trade route and provided important revenue, and Nasser, who had come to power in a *coup d'état* in 1954, wanted more of it.

At the end of October, Israel, Britain and France invaded Egypt and occupied parts of the canal but were forced into a humiliating withdrawal when the United Nations refused to support the action. Saudi Arabia imposed an oil embargo on exports to France and Britain.

Absent since 1950, petrol rationing was re-introduced from the end of November 1956 and lasted to May 1957. Queues at the pumps opened the door to a new breed of tiny fuel-sipping car, the 'bubble car' (see p.45).

This 1956 Rover T3 gas-turbine car was the first the company had shown at Earls Court, but its third prototype. It had a rear-mounted engine, four-wheel drive and a fibreglass body. The twin-shaft engine developed 110bhp at 52,000rpm. (Mirrorpix)

Fuel economy did not trouble Rover, which by the mid 1950s was at the forefront of British car engineering with its experimental gas-turbine cars. The gas turbine had come directly from the development of the jet engine. It sucks in large amounts of slow, cold air at the front, compresses and heats it and exhausts fast hot air at the back. In a jet engine the air provides forward thrust, in a car it propels a driveshaft. Rover had scored a world first in 1950 with Jet 1, a two-seater built on the basis of a Rover 75. More a jet engine on wheels than a car, it was tested up to 152mph at engines speeds of an incredible 50,000rpm. The T3 was the first turbine car it had shown at Earls Court, with a smaller rear-mounted turbine, and a purpose-designed fibreglass coupé body shell.

THE BUBBLE CAR BOOM

When British motorists panicked at the return of petrol rationing during the 1956 Suez crisis, a supply of tiny three-wheeled fuel-sipping cars was ready from Germany. Three wheelers were not classed as cars, but whilst banished from Earls Court they made a big impact on British motoring.

Encouraged as a way to quickly rebuild Germany's automobile industry, they owed much to motorcycles, with their single-cylinder air-cooled engines driving the rear wheel. The best known was the Bayerische Motoren Werke (BMW) Isetta, made under licence from Italian manufacturer Iso. Its shape earned it the name of 'bubble' car and the name stuck to all of its kind. Engines were a mere 245 and 295cc. A single front door not being a good idea in a crash, they all came with a sunroof escape route.

A number of German aircraft manufacturers used their skills for microcars. Messerschmitt's three-wheeled KR175 was one of the first in 1953, adapted from an invalid car design. Two people sat in line under a canopy not unlike a fighter plane. The Heinkel had a front-hinged door like the BMW. It was made under licence in Ireland and Britain as a Trojan.

Some four-wheeled German microcars made it to Earls Court in 1957, the oddest of which was the Zündapp Janus, made by aircraft manufacturer Dornier, with a centrally mounted engine and two pairs of seats which faced backwards and forwards (cue mother-in-law seat jokes). The Goggomobil was a pretty little coupé in miniature.

The tiny four-wheelers and British Meadows Frisky also caught the eyes of many at the 1957 show. Meadows was better known as a supplier of automotive, marine and industrial engines. Microcars were usually ugly boxes but Frisky's designer, Captain Raymond Flower, had gone to Italian stylist Giovanni Michelotti who produced a design with gullwing doors for the March 1957 Geneva show. By October it had lost the gullwing doors, been restyled and had a larger Villiers engine of 324cc to be sold as the Frisky Saloon and the Frisky Sport convertible. Although praised by the press, it was only produced fitfully by several owners until 1961, at one point becoming a three-wheeler.

Chugging away before and after the bubble car was the very minimal Bond Minicar, a three-wheeler from Preston produced since 1948 and which tried to look like a real car. Having three wheels was crucial. British laws allowed you to drive a three-wheeled car if you had a motorcycle licence (which many people did before widespread car ownership) and it attracted very low road tax if it weighed 500kg or less. This concession lasted until 2001. The 1957 Bond Minicar was propelled by a 197cc Villiers motorcycle engine sitting above a single front wheel which also steered. Bond dropped its price to compete with the bubbles: '£279, 85mpg, 50mph top speed and £5 road tax!' Too big to compare to a bubble car, the Reliant Regal was a van-based three-wheeler with an engine which could trace its lineage back to the 1920s Austin 7.

Although petrol rationing only ran from the end of November 1956 to May 1957, some motorists retained a taste for bubble cars and for a dependable 50mpg plus. Loved by cartoonists, they were brightly coloured parcels of fun – albeit slow, noisy and not a good place to be in an accident.

The boom in these strange, noisy and above all German minicars was too much for BMC's Leonard Lord to stand. In *Automobile Design: Great Designers and their Work*, Mini designer Alec Issigonis recalled him saying: 'God damn these bloody awful bubble-cars. We must drive them out of the streets by designing a proper miniature car.'

The bubble car was a spent force by the time the Mini arrived in summer 1959. A vastly more mature and sophisticated proposition, the Mini's famously foolish low price (meaning it lost money for its makers) rendered buying a crude bubble car pointless. A Morris Mini Minor or Austin 7 could be yours for £497 in 1960, a three-wheeled Heinkel £389, a Frisky £392 and a four-wheeled Goggomobil £467.

Notably tall actor Cary Grant extracts himself from a BMW Isetta bubble car. It was accessed by a single front door and windscreen on which the steering column hinged. (BMW)

The SMMT Motor Show enjoyed years of royal patronage – here the Queen Mother is delighted by a Vauxhall. (Vauxhall Heritage)

Away from the public, dealers and guests could relax in this riverside bar. Well, a bar with a picture of a river. (Vauxhall Heritage)

By the late 1950s Triumph's TR2 had become the TR3 and a respectable competition car. (Vauxhall Heritage)

How to make the interior look big – tiny passengers in a Vauxhall Victor. (Vauxhall Heritage)

1957

Most new models having been launched earlier in the year, the most significant British car to debut at the 1957 show was the Lotus Elite.

In the previous ten years Lotus Engineering of Hornsey, North London, had grown from Colin Chapman's home-built Austin Seven Special to a builder of formidable race cars and self-assembly kits for enthusiasts.

Lotus Engineering had only moved downstairs from the accessories section in 1956 and the Elite's completion was so last minute it didn't make the 1957 show catalogue. It was an audacious bid for the big-time, with a unitary (chassis-less) body made entirely of fibreglass and a sophisticated Coventry Climax race-derived engine. Chapman was determined that the Elite be seen at the 1957 show, but the first moulds were only ready that August and paint was still drying on the car the night before opening, when he broke the only windscreen. The correct Coventry Climax engine was too late so a Lotus Eleven engine was used and the show Elite was not a runner, but, finished in two-tone silver and gunmetal, it looked sensational. The 1957 show stand should also have seen the debut of the Lotus Seven, but it was left unfinished at the works. The first production Elite was only delivered in December 1958 and with each following show it was noted how the finish continued to improve. Lightweight and aerodynamic, when tested, the Lotus Elite's fuel consumption of 29.5mpg at 100mph was astonishing. However, while accomplished and beautiful, it developed a reputation for fragility and sales quickly dived.

BMC had two little upmarket saloons to show: the Wolseley 1500 and the Riley 1.5, the latter a little more powerful. These were successfully rebodied and plusher versions of the Morris Minor intended to replace it at one time, but the Minor was showing no signs of flagging almost ten years on.

Having been mildly updated in 1955 as the Aston Martin DB2/4 Mk II and now with a 162bhp 3-litre engine, what was to be the last of the Aston Martin DB2 line, the DB Mk III, had been launched at the March Geneva Motor Show. It was not a DB3; that name belonged to the DB3S racing car with which it shared its front-end styling. But, as Aston experts like to point out, James Bond creator Ian Fleming got this wrong himself when he named Bond's first Aston in *Goldfinger* as a DB3.

The Standard Pennant of 1957 was a dressed-up Ten with tailfins and two-tone paint. Signs to the multiple eateries behind it. (Vauxhall Heritage)

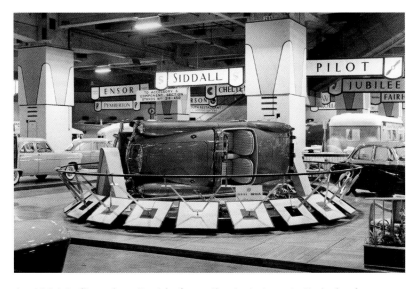

An MGA is flipped on its side for enthusiasts to note its lack of separate chassis. Then straight through to the caravans. (Vauxhall Heritage)

1958

Austin claimed it had created the 'Most advanced small car of the today' in 1958 but it didn't mean the Mini, which was still top secret. The Austin A40 was conventionally powered by the familiar 948cc A Series engine driving the rear wheels but its styling was certainly forward-looking and a complete contrast to the A35 it was designed to replace. BMC had engaged the services of Italian styling house Farina (Battista 'Pinin' Farina changed his surname to Pininfarina in 1961) to bring some continental sophistication to its products, and the A40 was the first of the line. In profile it was a foretaste of the modern hatchback, a 'two box' car with an engine and passenger section but no 'third box' of a boot, only an almost flat rear window above a tailgate. This latched downwards to reveal the luggage space and a later version, the Countryman, was near enough a hatchback, with an opening top window and fold-down rear seats. The A40 lasted well until 1967.

Although the looks of its DB range had once been said to have inspired Italian designers, Aston Martin had finally gone to Touring of Milan for its latest model, the beautiful DB4, an all-new car with a new tubular chassis constructed on the *Superleggera* (super-light) principle of an alloy body over a tubular frame, and a new 249bhp 3.7-litre twin-cam six-cylinder engine tamed by four-wheel disc brakes. Yours for £3,976, it would set the direction for Astons of the next decade. The last DB Mk III was built in 1959.

Owing nothing to Italian styling, the little bug-eyed Austin-Healey Sprite was the second sports car to wear the badge and had delighted enthusiasts since its May 1958 introduction. The well-established 948cc A Series engine was tuned to give 42½bhp instead of 37, thanks to twin carburettors with stronger valves and bearings to cope. This was paired with a four-speed gearbox with a short-shift gear lever. Responsive steering was supplied by the Morris Minor's rack-and-pinion set-up.

Manufacturing cost and weight were reduced by Austin-Healey doing away with door handles and winding windows (detachable side screens), and there was no separate boot lid. Two headlamps were perched atop the single-piece bonnet. They had been designed to sit flush and be raised with a lever but complexity and US headlamp height regulations meant they stayed upright in pods, bug-eyed or frog-eyed, as the car was soon nicknamed.

Aside from the glassfibre three-cylinder Berkley or the Austin-engined Turner 950 Sports, there was no competition in the 1.0-litre sports car market and, according to Healey expert Jon Pressnell, at £679 tax paid in May 1958 it was only £27 more than Austin A35 de Luxe, barely making BMC a profit. A hit at home and in America, the charming Frogeye Sprite ran to nearly 50,000 examples, largely unchanged until 1961, when it was restyled front and rear (with an opening boot) to become both the new Austin-Healey Sprite and MG Midget. The 'Spridgets' would enjoy a long life – though plenty said too long – the MG lasting until 1980.

After the show, the newspaper cuts were full of the usual boastful numbers, with 50,000 more visitors claimed than 1957's attendance of 534,222. Ford described it as the busiest show on record, Standard Triumph proclaimed that the hire-purchase terms announced before the show after the relaxation of credit controls had resulted in a substantial increase in stand and showroom visitors. Rover had to pull one of its 60s off the stand to make room for the crowds wanting to see the new 3-Litre.

1959

The last Motor Show of the 1950s was opened by the new prime minister, Harold Macmillan. His ministers were busy. The first stretch of British motorway – 8 miles of the M6 near Preston – had opened in December 1958, and the new Minister of Transport, Ernest Marples, was about to open the first 61.5 miles of the M1 and start the motorway age.

Having been launched in August and September respectively, Earls Court 1959 was the public's first chance to see BMC's new baby cars, the Austin Seven and Morris Mini-Minor, and an all-new Ford Anglia.

Slightly scared of the audacious Alec Issigonis Mini, with a transversely mounted A Series engine driving the front wheels and rubber-cone suspension, BMC attempted to link the Austin version (the pair separated by trim only) to the 1920s Austin Seven and link the Morris to the well-loved Minor. But only the Mini tag stuck.

It offered an incredible ratio of passenger space within the overall volume and was famously revealed to the media in late August at Longbridge. This fell to Tony Ball, a BMC rising star taken on as an engineering apprentice at Austin in 1951. By late 1958 he was personal assistant to the sales director Jim Penrose. 'I had reached a point where Sir Leonard Lord and Alec Issigonis invited me into the holy of holies, the design studio, pulled back the curtain and there was the Mini,' Tony told the author in 2015:

> And they said to me 'what do you think of this car young man?' I'd never seen a car like it before and the word that came into my head was magic. They said 'good, what would you do if we gave you the task of launching this car?' Thinking on my feet I said if they could let me have five hundred pounds I'd like to build a giant magician's top hat and put the car inside the top hat.
>
> I did the classic filling up of the car with all the luggage I could find, my wife and my eldest child, three of the biggest men I could find and a lady with two dogs. I came out looking like Fred Astaire on acid, waved the magic wand and said, 'Today ladies and gentleman, we're going to show you something unique and revolutionary, an act of magic in car design.'

At Earls Court, Mr Ball's 'wizardry on wheels' was illustrated by a Mini missing one half to reveal the ratio of engine to passenger space, a show trick BMC would often use in years to come.

The Earls Court Ford Anglia floated on an electrically undulating carpet. The most novel feature was not its ride but its nearly flat reverse-rake rear window, an idea already used in Detroit, which kept it clear in rain, allowed a large boot opening and created more rear passenger headroom.

Its 997cc engine was rear wheel-drive as usual and Ford had to defend its conventional engineering against the Mini, even to its own dealers, but the Anglia 105E was an instant sales success. In 1960, 191,000 were produced, then a record for a British car. By contrast, hampered by early production problems including well-publicised water leaks, just 116,000 Minis were produced the same year.

Taxis form a typical jam around a wet Earls Court during the 1959 show. (Mirrorpix)

Police protection for Prime Minister Harold Macmillan as Ford's Sir Patrick Hennessey explains the virtues of the 1959 Anglia's reverse-slope screen. A booth behind offers fruitless test drives. (Ford Motor Company Ltd)

Late August 1959 and Tony Ball has just revealed the Mini, containing, left to right: his wife Ruth and son Kevin, Austin fleet sales manager Stan Ellison, management trainee Sandy Baird, road tester Alf Depper, Mrs Depper and her two poodles, plus luggage. (Mirrorpix)

Actress Eve Arnold perches in the new Sunbeam Alpine on press day 1959. The man on the phone is listening to the car's virtues being extolled. (Rootes, courtesy of Coventry History Centre)

The Mini, of course, became a timeless classic, while the Anglia's styling would become dated. Nonetheless, the Ford 105E engine went on to become one of motoring's most successful power units and the mainstay of many British sports and racing cars.

There was an equally interesting small car from Triumph. In April 1959 Standard Triumph had unveiled the Herald, different yet again to the Mini and Anglia with smart Italian styling from Michelotti. Designed to replace the Standard Ten and using its 948cc engine and transmission, it appeared to have gone technically backward by the use of body sections bolted to a separate chassis. This was simply because that was the only way Standard Triumph could get it into mass production.

The Herald's construction was the end result of BMC buying Fisher & Ludlow and Ford Briggs in 1953 to guarantee supply of its bodyshells, to the detriment of others. This had led smaller Standard Triumph into the purchase of Mulliners in Birmingham but also other companies around the country, including Halls Engineering

in Liverpool. The Herald, in development since 1956, had to be made from several body sections coming together in Coventry from different factories, which could lead to some rattles and large panel gaps.

If it seemed archaic, Triumph turned this system of construction to its advantage as it as easy to add variants. The Herald started as a two-door saloon, convertible and coupé, then a van. The chassis was also the basis for the six-cylinder Triumph Vitesse and the Spitfire and GT6 sports cars. The one-piece bonnet swing forwards for great engine access and Triumph advertising often showed driver and passengers sitting atop a bare chassis boasting of its sturdiness. It also allowed a notably tight turning circle: 'tighter than a London taxi'.

Citroën's new British small car for 1960s was to be an abject failure. Having kept it secret until 17 October for an unveiling at the factory, Citroën cars of Slough introduced their very own design of small car at the 1959 show, the Bijou, French for 'jewel'. On the surface it was a pleasantly styled fibreglass two-door car but underneath it was pure Citroën 2CV. After struggling since 1953 to sell the 'tin snail' to British buyers, Slough decided to end 2CV assembly in 1959 and hoped that the Bijou would not only use up the last few chassis but become a British model in its own right. The bodyshell was styled by Peter Kirwan-Taylor, who had penned the Lotus Elite and the Bijou was marketed as a smart shopping car for *Madame*. It would have been in trouble had it ventured beyond the town; the 2CV engine might have been enlarged to a whole 425cc, but the Bijou was all out at 45mph. *Motorsport* called it a funny small car 'with a fan in its nose, an ugly 2/4-seater plastic body and an enormous single-spoke steering wheel cribbed from its elegant sister the DS19'.

After the show the prototype was destroyed and the front grille enlarged, but the Bijou was doomed to failure from the start. With purchase tax, the price at Earls Court 1959 was £674 when the most expensive Mini was £536. Just 211 Bijous were sold until 1962.

For the larger family, the second Farina design for BMC arrived in late 1958, a large four-door saloon with distinctive tail fins. BMC ran riot with its brands. The Farina saloons wore Austin, Morris, MG, Riley, Wolseley and Vanden Plas badges in the following decade with four or six-cylinder engines.

Popping out like sausages, each car would get its own launch a few months after the last with only a badge, a grille and some interior trim to tell it apart. It stretched even the patience of the loyal British journals. Yet these underpowered, over-bodied simple saloons took pride of place on many British driveways and on taxi ranks for the best part of the decade: their vast boots swallowing everything for the annual traffic jam to the seaside. They were sturdy too; in the 1970s the battering ram of choice for 'banger' racers.

Rootes was showing a pretty new Sunbeam Alpine, this time with token rear seats only. Underneath it was based on the Sunbeam Rapier but motoring writers sniffily liked to say it was based on the Hillman Husky floor pan, deeming it not quite fast enough or too heavy to be a proper sports car like an MG. As the Hillman range gained larger engines, so did the Alpine, moving from 1.5 to 1.6 litres a year later. It was the first car Sean Connery drove in a Bond car chase for 1962's *Dr No*.

The Rolls Royce Silver Cloud II appeared little changed but its new all-alloy V8 engine replaced the long-lived six-cylinder unit and would last until the 1990s.

If Britain wanted to sell to the Soviet Union, it had to admit its goods, and the Moskvitch and Volga saloons were seen at a British motor show for the first time, proudly shown to Mr Macmillan by Soviet ambassador Mr Malik, said *The Times*. It was noted that Russian cars of this era appeared to ape the American capitalist excesses of chrome and fins.

As the 1950s bowed out, the death toll of smaller British manufacturers was striking, as the only way to survive became mergers or takeovers if the product or factory was attractive enough to a bigger company.

With Sir Bernard and Lady Docker ousted, Daimler had two last cars to note for the 1959 show. The styling of its new two-seater SP250 divided opinion, with its fish-mouthed grille and prominent rear fins. It had first been seen at the New York Auto Show that spring, where it was named the Daimler Dart, until Dodge pointed out that name was already theirs. Rapidly developed, the SP250 (after its respected new 2.5-litre V8 engine) had a fibreglass body, which sat on a chassis largely copied from the Triumph TR2. Despite early reliability problems, it was a potential 120mph car and this famously earned it work as a Metropolitan police chase car.

Daimler's independence was, however, coming to an end. Sir William Lyons, head of Jaguar, had been eyeing up Daimler's ready-made extra factory space and Daimler became part of Jaguar in 1960. With the E-Type Jaguar in prospect, Lyons was reluctant to develop the SP250 further. Daimler hoped to sell at least 3,000 SP250s a year, but only 2,645 were built to 1964.

The Majestic Major was the 1958 Majestic with a 4561cc version of the V8, giving much less stately progress than its funeral-car looks suggested. The Majestic limousines appeared until 1968, after which the Daimler badge adorned a Jaguar-derived limousine and denoted top-range Jaguars.

Having introduced the Sapphire 4-Litre the previous year, Armstrong-Siddeley continued to trail in the wake of Jaguar. It had designed the engine for the Humber Super Snipe, and Rootes had passed it the task of assembling the Alpine, but by 1960 the name was gone, as the parent group, Hawker-Siddeley, had merged with Bristol Aeroplanes and decided to concentrate on aero matters. Standard Triumph was acquired by commercial-vehicle giant Leyland in 1961, spelling the swift end of the Standard name.

Country sights and
smells in the hall at the
Royal Smithfield show
1970 and fortifications
at the 1972 Royal
Tournament. Both were
Earls Court regulars.
(Olympia/LMA)

Opposite: The swimming pool provided a
harbour for the Boat Show for decades.
Here it is in 1971 with a Chinese theme.
Note how the topmost floor was screened
off when not used. (Olympia/LMA)

The 1946 Bristol 400 was the aero manufacturer's first car; its swooping lines derived from a pre-war BMW. Bristol established a reputation for quality and their cars outlasted most of their rivals'. (Deborah Kidd)

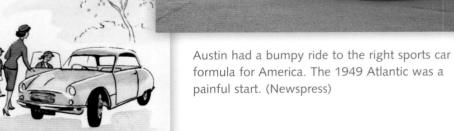

Austin had a bumpy ride to the right sports car formula for America. The 1949 Atlantic was a painful start. (Newspress)

THE
UNIQUE
CITROEN
BIJOU

The Citroën Bijou, a 2CV re-bodied in Slough, was the least successful small car debut of the 1959 show. (Giles Chapman Picture Library)

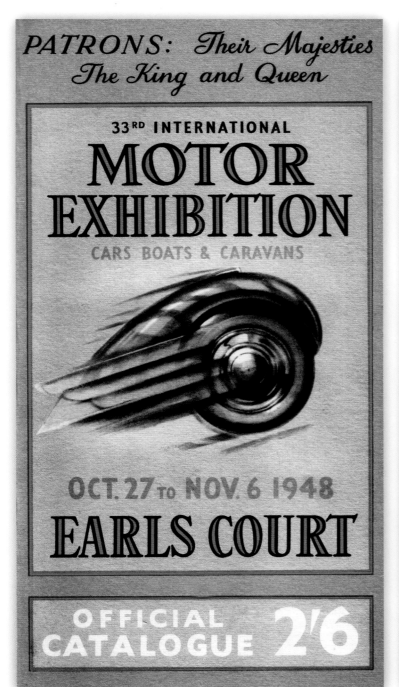

Show guides and posters artwork reflected the design of the period – the building itself often featured. (SMMT, courtesy of Coventry History Centre)

A full page in a motoring magazine's show guide was the place to be if you could afford it, or you could buy the cover itself, possible with *The Autocar* until the 1960s. (Author's collection)

1961 and Ford's star is the Classic (forefront and middle). September had seen the announcement of a coupé version, the Consul Capri 335, at the far end of the stand. (Olympia/LMA)

BUILD UP; KNOCK DOWN

By 1960 the number of fixtures hosted at Earls Court had jumped to fourteen a year, compared to seven in 1950, although some were bi-annual. By 1965 this had swelled to twenty-seven distinct exhibitions, some trade but most public, with unusual combinations if each didn't take the entire venue. Thus the Effluent and Water Treatment exhibition was teamed with Laboratory Apparatus and Automatic Vending between 29 March and 2 April.

Earls Court Ltd let out the halls to an exhibition-organising company, which then sublet stand space to individual exhibiting companies. Each exhibitor would commission their own supplier to design and build their stand. For every exhibition there would be many different stand-building companies working simultaneously. Earls Court also ran its own.

All this could get very political. In the late 1960s friend of the author Bob Dilley was working in the publicity department of Stanley Bridges, the British power tool subsidiary of the American Stanley Tool Corporation which exhibited at the annual Building Exhibition: 'One year I was observing the building of our stand and, as I was young and inexperienced, decided to help by putting up one of our exhibition panels,' he recalls:

> As soon as I went to pick up a hammer I was immediately stopped by my very agitated manager. He explained that, as I was not a union member, I could cause a strike not only by our own stand fitters but by the entire work force working on the exhibition. In those days the 'closed shop' was still legal and you couldn't work manually without a union card.

Every show had to be in and out as soon as possible, even if, like the Motor Show, there seemed a comfortable gap. Again taking 1965 as an example, the Caravan Show finished on 2 October and the cars were ready to meet the public on the 20th. 'The stand fitters were normally given four or five days to build the exhibition, but only a few hours to take it down,' Bob remembers. 'So at the end of the last day, the whole of Earls Court was flattened in what seemed a couple of minutes, but was more likely an hour or so. A truly awesome sight!'

The 1967 Furniture Show, a less famous but regular Earls Court fixture. These simple stands would come down in hours. (Olympia/LMA)

Opposite: Well-developed electric cars were seldom seen at the show but Ford's 1967 Comuta was a serious attempt at a viable electric car that lost its spark as its maker lost interest. (Ford Motor Company Ltd)

SALES AND THE SHOW

While you could inspect the latest cars at the Earls Court Motor Show, you couldn't buy them. From its outset in 1937 it was an exhibition of goods and, by regulation, nothing could be bought from the stands until the show closed, unless it was delivered from the company warehouse.

You were directed only to badged stand personnel who would take your details and feed them through to the local dealer, who would then get in touch, offer a test drive and agree a price. If a purveyor of luxury cars had a celebrity like Peter Sellers 'buying' a car at the show, the deal had most likely already been done or was about to be.

BMC make the cars that make sense.

Like all other manufacturers, BMC sent you to a showroom if you tried to buy a car at Earls Court. (Author's collection)

If you wanted a BMC car in the 1950s and '60s it had such a vast spread that the chance of an available neighbourhood dealer was high. By 1962 BMC's combined total of Austin, Morris, Wolseley, Riley and MG dealers ran to over 5,700. 'Direct sales weren't formally allowed but when we had an enquiry we fed to the dealers on the same day,' Tony Ball recalls. 'We'd just call them, give them the name and address and get them to do a good deal or put the name on the waiting list.'

Former Rover engineer John Baumber recalls this happening to his family: 'My first Motor Show visit was in the mid-sixties when I was a teenager when my parents were looking to buy a new car. Then you could actually place an order at the show and there was a car ready to try brought to the house the next day. It was an Austin A110 Westminster.'

Yet even though the show itself caused gridlock you could ask some carmakers for a test drive at Earls Court. 'We used to try and run test drives in there as well, for goodness' sake,' said Ford's Harry Calton. 'You always had a number of demo cars at Earls Court, with test drivers. If a customer asked, could they have a test drive, all they did, particularly at the weekend, or Saturday in particular, was drive out through the front gate and join the queue.'

Piles of sales catalogues or brochures were a daily feature of the mass-market carmaker stands, plundered by those with neither the intention nor the ability to buy a new car. Periodic attempts to crack down were doomed. If you were a car-mad teenage boy a major thrill of a Motor Show visit was to come away with as many brochures as possible.

Of course this generosity varied by the status of manufacturer. Small boys and ordinary adults were not going to come away with Ferrari or Rolls-Royce catalogues. This was a constant, as motoring journalist and 1974 teenage visitor Richard Bremner remembers:

It was quite easy with the big selling brands BL [British Leyland], Ford, Vauxhall and Chrysler. I think they were reasonably amenable to spotty kids asking for stuff – one day they might buy cars. I also got Lotus brochures, but no high-end ones but maybe that's because I was too timid to ask. I remember just feeling guilty all the time because I had absolutely no intention at least at that point of buying anything. But I came away with quite a haul, which I still have.

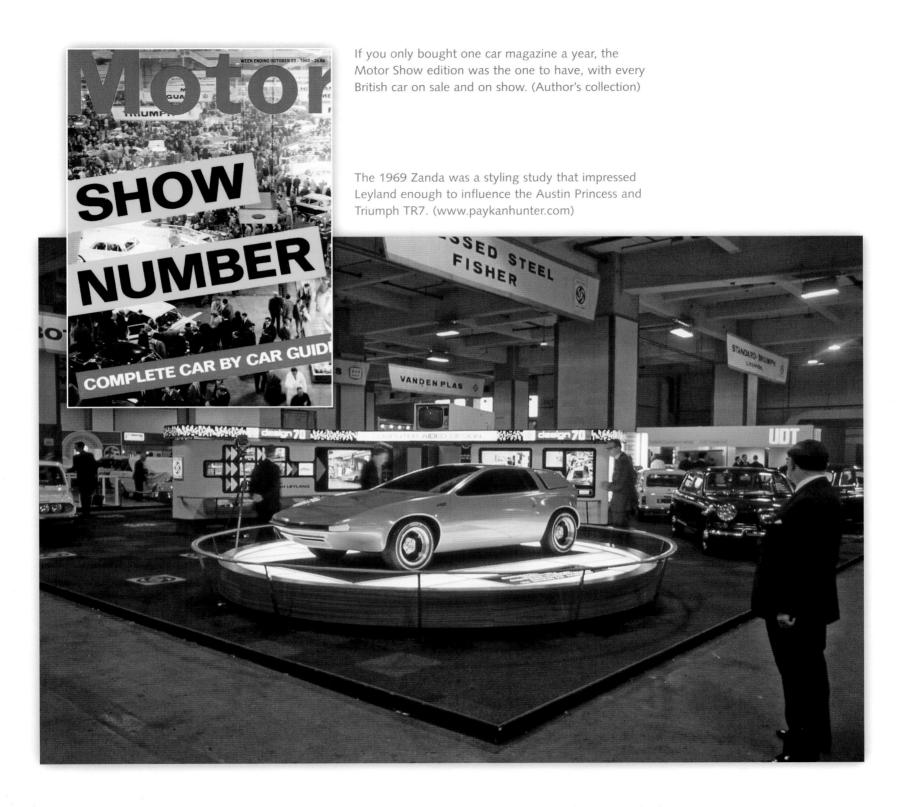

If you only bought one car magazine a year, the Motor Show edition was the one to have, with every British car on sale and on show. (Author's collection)

The 1969 Zanda was a styling study that impressed Leyland enough to influence the Austin Princess and Triumph TR7. (www.paykanhunter.com)

The Triumph 2500 and the Rover 3500, once direct rivals, face each other across the walkway in 1969. By then they had become part of the giant British Leyland group. (Olympia/LMA)

Beyond the acclaimed Jaguar XJ at the 1970 show sits the
first-generation Range Rover, already established as a car for the
smart set. (LAT)

The 1973 ACE 3000 ME made a splash at the 1973 show,
returning with promises it would go into production with each
show until 1979. (Giles Chapman Picture Library)

4 EXPANSION
1960–69

After the celebrated debuts of 1959, 1960 was a year for Britain's major manufacturers to sit back and hope for big profits. This optimism was short lived as the country's shaky grip on export markets began to loosen.

As was the tradition, companies still contrived news of big orders to be announced at the Earls Court show start, 19 October. The hire-car business was expanding in 1960s Britain and Wellbeck Motors ordered 600 Fords for £430,000 and Godfrey Davis 1,000 vehicles for £500,000. Autohall Car Hire apparently snapped up 750 Anglias, Consuls and Populars on opening day.

By 1960 it was somewhat of a tradition for *The Autocar*'s show review to be written firmly tongue-in-cheek by the well-respected Ronald 'Steady' Barker who would tour preview day accompanied by staff cartoonist Gordon Horner and a range of fictitious characters who were allowed to be rude about the cars. An unseen secretary called Miss Trubshaw took notes and made baffled remarks. For 1960 she, Barker and Horner were joined by Horner's bemused and flustered Uncle George who was about to finally change his 1937 car and wanted them to help choose a replacement (he failed to do so having been distracted by the showgirls):

Everyone said it would be a dull show, and, as we would find almost nothing new to talk about this time, why bother to try? Why? Because it takes much less than nothing to stop Horner and Barker talking; anyone who doesn't want to listen can just turn to page 725.

19 October 1960: kicking off a decade of industrial unrest, protestors demonstrate against redundancy sackings at the Cricklewood coachbuilding factory of Thrupp and Maberly as well as the credit squeeze. (Mirrorpix)

An appearance at Earls Court did not guarantee success. Not a single order was taken for the 1960 Lea-Francis Lynx. (Giles Chapman Picture Library)

The floor was open to the Lea-Francis Leaf-Lynx to create a short-lived sensation. Once a producer of well-respected sports cars and saloons, the Coventry company had given up car production in 1952 to produce jigs and tools but in 1959 decided to revive the car name to avoid going under completely. Kenneth Benfield, a local building contractor and its biggest shareholder, became chairman and commissioned a car for the 1960 Motor Show. The hurried styling was intended to evoke 'two cigars in a catamaran shape', according to Jon Pressnell's 1987 recounting of the story. Sketched by the company's publicist (also a cartoonist and pub comedian), two prototypes were thrown together for the show, one with a 2.5-litre Ford Zephyr engine, another with no engine at all. They were painted in a metallic lilac pastel shade, which looked peculiar under the Earls Court lighting. Barker wrote: 'When Horner asked a man on the stand wearing a Lea-Francis tie if he really thought this was the kind of Lea-Francis Britons would like, he said never mind, they were certainly the kind Americans liked.' Critics likened it to a bathtub and not a single order was taken at the show. Only three cars were ever built.

Although bubble cars were still being manufactured, the German motor industry was decisively into its 'proper' car phase and into a time of mergers and takeovers. The three-cylinder DKW Junior was a crisply styled small saloon; DKW itself was part of the Auto Union GmbH – now better known as Audi – which was taken over by Daimler-Benz in 1958 and would be bought by Volkswagen in 1965. The critics were impressed by the new 'Grosse Borgward' limousine with its air suspension, but it lasted only ten months; the firm folded in 1961. Mercedes carried magnificently on with its 220S saloon; the SE version was fuel injected. Pathé News predicted accurately that the 'Simms petrol injector may replace carburettors'.

The exhibition building itself had some expensive running repairs: the 1960–61 accounts showed £21,000 to refurbish one escalator, and the other five would cost £75,000 later in 1961.

1961

There was more motoring gloom when October 1961 rolled around. The BBC's *Panorama* had reported on Britain's plummeting exports to the USA (from 36.8 per cent of exports in 1959 to 8.2 per cent in 1961) and its emphasis on Volkswagen success had displeased new BMC chairman George Harriman. On 17 October, the night before the show opened, Sir Reginald Rootes announced that he had sacked 8,000 workers (out of 10,000) due to an unofficial stoppage at the Acton works, with talks between the company and the unions for a return to work having broken down. The British motor industry was set for two decades of industrial turmoil.

The public's interest in new cars continued unabated; the 1961 show would close with 578,034 through the turnstiles, up 149,497 on 1960. It was making the crowds of the 1950s look like a walk in the park. 'In the '60s, Saturdays became so crowded that you couldn't get on the stand,' Harry Calton of Ford recalls:

If Chelsea were playing at home we used to take it in turns to go and watch the football match on Saturday afternoon. We'd have a sort of skeleton staff on the stand and then those who did duty on Saturday afternoon would then go home. Those who'd been to the football match would come back again for the evening shift.

Where would all these people eat? If you didn't want to leave the building, in 1961 showgoers could choose from five restaurants, a cafeteria, three tea and coffee buffets, a coffee and sandwich lounge, and a further twenty arena bars and five lounge bars plus numerous vending machines around the fringes. The entire contract for catering at Earls Court was held by the Peter Merchant Company (Merchant had helped set up Little Chef roadside restaurants). There were seventeen private dining rooms for exhibitors. The Alpine Restaurant naturally had murals of said mountains, plus full table service. According to an internal magazine feature from Peter Merchant, a wine cellar furnished the restaurants and stands with 5,000 bottles of gin and 4,000 bottles of whisky during the 1961 Motor Show. Even with all this choice there was going to be some queuing. The Popular Cafeteria could seat 700 and on the first Saturday catered for 7,000. None of this was going to be cheap and visitors had long moaned about the prices. 'Meals at Earls Court have rarely been notable except for discomfort and expense,' *The Autocar* had grumped ten years previously. 'Staff members of this journal contemplated with awe a buffet on the second mezzanine floor in which one round of chicken sandwiches cost 4s 6 a piece [£5.31 in 2014 prices]; for 3s 6d a round they could have eaten smoked salmon.'

Great British cars kept on coming. Jaguar had already stolen the motoring year with the introduction of the E-Type, announced as a coupé and convertible at the Geneva Motor Show in March, and at first for export only, going on British sale in July. Its lines, which then and now make it one of the most beautiful cars in the world, were developed from the C- and D-Type sports racers, its 3.8-litre six-cylinder XK engine boasted 265bhp and promised a top speed of 150mph for £2,036 for the open two-seater or £100 more for the coupé.

Jaguar also pulled off a grand announcement at the show with the very big Jaguar Mark X (or Mark 10) saloon. This 16ft leviathan contained the E-Type's independent rear suspension and its engine for high-speed luxury cruising. It was aimed straight at America, where Jaguar dealers were said to already have 1,000 on order.

This was bad news for the Lagonda Rapide, which had been announced at the September Paris Motor Show. David Brown's Aston Martin company had discontinued Lagonda saloons in 1958 and the name re-emerged on a saloon styled by Touring of Italy with a 4-litre version of the Aston BD4 six-cylinder engine. Not

Jaguar boss Sir William Lyons with the Jaguar E-Type during its launch in Geneva, March 1961. With an eye to America first, British buyers had to wait until later in the year. (Jaguar)

In 1962 Ford staged a mini motor show at its Regent Street showroom for its new Cortina – more room than the doomed Classic for less money and destined to rule the sales charts into the 1980s. (Ford Motor Company Ltd)

regarded as terribly attractive, its £5,251 price was off-putting when the Jaguar only cost £2,392. Records vary, but only fifty-four or fifty-five Rapides were built in 1964 and the name became dormant for a decade.

BMC was showing the new MG Midget and Austin-Healey Sprite, posh Minis, the Riley Elf and the Wolesley Hornet. With all its mechanical parts at the front, BMC had realised that you could stick many different things on the back of a Mini. A van and estate had appeared in 1960, and the Elf and Hornet gained extra length and protruding boots with proper bootlids, unlike the regular Mini's flip-down item. The inside was carpeted and given better seats, and the open dashboard was filled in with a wooden fascia. This pair of genteel Minis lasted until 1969 largely unchanged. Also at Earls Court, Zagato exhibited a small coupé based on a Mini van platform, which failed to translate into production.

Of rather more interest to enthusiasts was the Morris Mini Cooper, announced that September and to become as much of a motoring legend as the E-Type. Early on, racers had realised that the Mini's superb handling cried out for more power and, though never planned, BMC collaborated with racing team name John Cooper to increase the engine size to 997cc and 55bhp with twin carburettors – displayed at the show in a see-through plastic Perspex bonnet. A Morris version came first then an Austin. In its later 1275cc form it proved to be a giant-killing rally star.

This was a significant year for Renault, making the switch to front-wheel drive and a true hatchback with the Renault 4L, its versatility demonstrated to the press by two ladies hauling luggage and a pram in and out of it. In the same year production of the Renault Dauphine started at Acton, but it would be the last British Renault. The little 4 was to become a French national treasure, running to over 8 million by 1994.

The Chrysler Turboflite was an attention-grabbing show car (or 'ideacar') with a roof which raised vertically to admit occupants, but it did in fact have an advanced engine – a gas turbine – which, like Rover, the company was then seriously experimenting with. As Pathé noted, one of the advantages was that a gas turbine could run on any liquid fuel – petrol, kerosene, diesel, heating oil or a combination of them. The downsides were high manufacturing costs and poor fuel consumption. Gas-turbine cars also demanded a completely different driving style and proved to be a dead end.

A conventional transatlantic engine – a Canadian-built 5.4-litre Chrysler V8 – could be found in the Bristol 407. It was the first of the Anglo-American Bristols, and other small-scale luxury car makers would contribute to a trend for dropping a reliable, fast and easily serviced American engine into their cars rather than struggle with their own designs. Jensen switched from Austin engines to a Chrysler V8 for the CV-8 in 1962. In smaller sports cars the effect was 'hairy'. Aimed more at boosting American sales, in 1962 AC squeezed a Ford V8 into the Ace to create the mighty Cobra, and in 1964 Rootes did the same to create the Sunbeam Tiger from the Alpine; TVR created the Griffith from the Grantura.

Ford of Britain's big news at the 1961 show turned out to be one of its rare errors. The laboriously titled Consul Classic 315 had appeared in spring 1961. In development since 1956, this was a badly needed model to fill a gap in the Ford range between the Anglia/Prefect and the Consul. Soon Ford knew it had laid an egg. Too heavy and too expensive to build, the Classic range was to be rapidly eclipsed by the Cortina the following year and discontinued in 1963; the related Capri coupé went in 1964.

Vauxhall was entering an era where its own stylists were breaking free from producing miniature versions of Detroit products. In the summer of 1961 the neatly styled 1508cc FB Series Victor had replaced the F Series of 1957, which had looked like a shrunken Pontiac (even sold alongside them for a time) and developed fame for rapid rust. While Ford of America was set to plough millions of dollars into creating a performance image, General Motors forbade Vauxhall very much sportiness. The Victor VX4-90 might have boasted 71.3bhp over the usual 48.5, had a rev counter, a floor-mounted gear change and even a side flash, but Vauxhall made no claims of sportiness.

1962

The British motor industry's eyes were firmly on Europe for 1962. 'Prophets are saying this is the last year outside the common market,' said comedian Bob Monkhouse, the breezy voiceover for Pathé News. The American market now meant little except sports car sales. European countries belonged to two trading groups, the Common Market (EEC) and the European Free Trade Area (EFTA). Germany,

The BMC 1100 was the Cortina's deadly rival throughout the 1960s. It is seen here in its 1962 MG guise. (BMIHT/Newspress)

way to the top of the domestic sales charts. The 1100 was Britain's best-selling car until supplanted by the Cortina in February 1967.

It was a vintage year for British sports car fans. Triumph had expanded its TR range into a TR4 in July 1961 and Earls Court 1962 brought a new competitor to the BMC 'Spridgets', the Triumph Spitfire 4, styled as the Herald had been by Michelotti and based on the Herald's chassis, its 1147cc engine upgraded to 63bhp. Triumph also continued to make the most of the Herald parts bin to create the Vitesse saloon and convertible with a 1.6-litre six-cylinder engine, unique in this size of car.

The MGA finally gave way to the MGB, the brand's first sports car with unitary construction and the 1798cc BMC B Series engine with 95bhp: launched as a smart convertible in July 1962. Like the Sunbeam Alpine, it majored in sturdiness and comfort with an

France and Italy, the major car-producing Europeans, belonged to the EEC, while Britain was in EFTA, whose members on the whole were smaller countries. The British motor industry wanted into the Common Market and the first application was made in 1962, but it was not to succeed until 1973, when the country was in a poor state to benefit.

The battle lines for supremacy of the British family car market had been set just before the 1962 show. August had seen the launch of BMC's Pininfarina-styled Morris 1100, a grown-up Mini with the same space-saving transverse engine and front-wheel drive plus fluid-filled Hydrolastic suspension. The next month came the Ford Cortina, rear-wheel drive with a 1200cc engine developed from the Anglia.

Ford of England had developed the Cortina in record time, its production costs ruthlessly screwed down, as a kind of slimmed-down Classic. The advertising copy was uninhibited in its promises of space, price and, above all, reliability.

The 1100 was smart and clever but the Cortina had a huge boot (as large as the new, more expensive Hillman Super Minx) and was easy to service and great to drive. Ford's preparation and planning also gave the Cortina a simple and compelling advantage over the 1100, which was slow to get into production. You could walk into a Ford dealer and buy one there and then. Both soon found their

'How to carry a big dog without letting him push you through the windscreen' – the 1962 Radford Countryman Bentley conversion surrendered the back seat to a cage for a posh pooch. (Mirrorpix)

Simca was going through an aquatic Motor Show phase with the new Simca 1000 in 1962. Don't mention rust. (Mirrorpix)

The pop-up headlamps were to become another Elan trademark, and bugbear. The space inside the front-chassis cross member was fully enclosed and used as a reservoir of air to power the headlamp opening, which was then closed by a spring catch. Getting the mechanism to work reliably took Lotus right up to the Elan's debut at Earls Court, but on the day they were wired to flash as they popped up (in less than a second) – a real crowd pleaser.

The snag was the price. The specialised, low-volume Elan 1500 was £1,499 fully built when an MGB was around £800, but it was £1,095 as a tax-free kit if you built it yourself. By now Lotus was a past master at making this much less daunting than it sounded. Buyers weren't allowed to have instructions because that would have been contrary to the regulations, so Lotus gave them pages from the workshop manual which explained how to dismantle it. The crafty buyer then' reversed the sequence. The dealer would then check the finished car over for any incorrectly fitted parts.

The Elan's desirability was cemented by weekly appearances on *The Avengers* TV show driven by Diana Rigg as Mrs Peel. In its various forms the Elan lasted until 1975, remaining a benchmark for sweet-handling sports cars for decades more.

1963

A new word was creeping into the 1960s: 'executive'. Poet John Betjeman wrote: 'I am a young executive. No cuffs than mine are cleaner; I have a Slimline brief-case and I use the firm's Cortina.'

If you were a young go-getting (on the whole male) business type then you needed an executive car. A contemporary saloon with up-to-date engineering, European styling and a 2-litre engine. A bit sporty, like the specialised sports saloons of the previous decades. In 1963 there were suddenly two fine executive cars, the Rover 2000 and the Triumph 2000.

A complete break from the upright 'Auntie' Rovers of the 1950s, the 2000's low styling had been previewed in the T4 gas-turbine car of 1961. Befitting the company's reputation for innovation, it featured many new features which earned it the first-ever Car of the Year title. Like the Citroën DS, it had fully detachable body panels bolted to a strong unitary construction base unit. The front suspension was compact enough to allow a wide engine bay for a gas turbine and

optional overdrive on its top gear that gave more relaxed cruising. Joined by a handsome GT version in 1965, the MGB would become Britain's best-selling sports car by dint of its eighteen-year lifespan with over 500,000 produced.

However, the sports car the real enthusiast lusted after in 1962 was the little Lotus Elan. There was much to please in its exotic specification. Its fibreglass body sat on a separate chassis holding the exciting new Ford-based twin overhead cam engine and a sophisticated rear independent suspension, which combined a supple ride with great handling. Fibreglass bumpers hid the join between the upper and lower panels, and also concealed a plastic foam and fibreglass sandwich capable of absorbing minor knocks.

the rear suspension was a sophisticated independent unit with a De Dion axle for great ride and handling, while all four wheels had disc brakes. The dashboard had echoes of modern Danish wood furniture while the rear seats were only shaped for two individuals in supreme leather-clad comfort. It was considered an extremely safe car, with seatbelts, head restraints and impact-absorbing interior parts.

More conservative but still smartly styled by Michelotti, Triumph's 2000 executive saloon boasted a six-cylinder engine from the last Standard Vanguard. Unlike the Rover, it was developed into an estate and was the first British car to receive standard – if troublesome – Lucas fuel injection in 1968, as the 2.5 PI.

Both the Rover and Triumph carried a prestige price premium over the traditional larger six-cylinder cars from Vauxhall and Ford, the Velox and the Zephyr Six. However, Ford had its own junior executive car ready for 1963, the 1.5-litre Corsair (which until a late stage was to have been called the Classic), developed in rapid time from the Cortina, lengthened with a new tail and a pointed nose resembling the latest Thunderbird. Just a little bit more fancy than a Cortina.

Walter Hayes, a former car journalist, had become Ford's public affairs director and saw an opportunity to add a bit of glamour to the Cortina at the show with the 'Ford Cortina GT modified by Ogle', a curious-looking fastback Cortina finished in metallic green. Racing driver Stirling Moss was seeking to carve out a new career following his near-fatal 1962 racing accident and made an association with British car design firm Ogle. The fastback Cortina was billed as Mr Moss's idea of a practical yet sophisticated GT car 'to carry four people comfortably, confidently, on 500 miles-a-day journeys with all the luggage they would need'. The conversion was contracted out to coachbuilder Harold Radford and every modern gadget was thrown at the interior, from a two-speaker radio with automatic aerial to an optional TV monitor. It remained a one-off.

With hindsight, the most industrially significant car at the 1963 show was Hillman's totally new Imp, displaying its unusual features with the help of vaguely Impish ladies and Perspex body panels. A belated response to the success of the Mini, the Imp had a rear-mounted engine driving the rear wheels when most European manufacturers were switching to front engines and front-wheel drive. But the engine was a sweet-spinning all-aluminium 875cc unit which could trace its lineage to a Coventry Climax racing engine, the throttle linkage controlled by air in a sealed system. It had a small boot in the

Model Caron Gardner sits inside a Hillman Imp built of Perspex to show its rear-engined layout interior at the 1963 show – it tried to take on the Mini and failed. (Mirrorpix)

front and the rear window opened as a hatchback to fold-flat rear seats. However, the Imp had been hastily developed and in real-life conditions the little engine overheated and the throttle air leaked.

It wasn't helped by its factory. As Britain's car industry continued to expand in the 1960s it found itself in need of more space. However, expansion for new models on existing sites was forbidden by the government, which 'encouraged' growth industries such as car makers to locate new plants in areas of high unemployment. Not only was the Imp all new, it was produced in an all-new factory at Linwood in Glasgow, next to the Pressed Steel complex. The location was some 300 miles away from Rootes's traditional home in Coventry and there was an inefficient traffic of components

The new Rover 2000 delights Carry On film actor Sid James and Rover demonstrator Auriol Mackeson-Sandbach slips off her shoes, 15 October 1963. (Mirrorpix)

assembled between the two locations, such as the engine. Coupling early reliability problems to these unpromising logistics was an increasingly militant workforce.

The Imp was developed into sportier Sunbeam and luxury Singer versions, became a creditable rally car and deserved better, but its early unreliability, poor sales and Linwood's troubles hastened the sale of Rootes to Chrysler later in the decade.

Vauxhall's 1963 re-entry into small cars, the Viva, seemed almost wilfully conservative but was destined for a much more successful life. Designed in parallel to its German cousin the Opel Kadett, the Viva had its rear wheels driven by a new 1057cc engine, front-wheel-drive having been studied and ruled out for both by parent company General Motors. Although it was rear-wheel drive, the Viva's boxy shape was designed to squeeze in as much passenger and luggage space as possible into its two-door style.

Made (successfully) in a new factory at Ellesmere Port near Liverpool, the most exciting thing that history seems to note about the first Viva is that it was the first British car to use an acrylic lacquer paint finish for a long-lasting shine.

BMC was busy shamelessly badge engineering the 1100 with new radiator grilles to become the Riley Kestrel or Wolseley 1100 and an extra carburettor to be the MG 1100. The Vanden Plas Princess 1100, however, was a cut above. Smartly latching onto the fashion for luxury minis from such brands as Radford, BMC had put its own coachbuilder Vanden Plas to work on the best-seller. Vanden Plas modified the rear tailfins and the front panel, adding a square grille and an opulent interior with Jaguar-like leather seats, polished wood picnic tables folding from the rear of the front seats and a great deal of soundproofing. At £895 in 1964 it was almost £200 more than an MG 1100 but established itself as a mini Rolls-Royce, remaining in production to 1974.

The Aston Martin DB5 replaced the successful DB4 in coupé and convertible form, visually similar but with faired-in headlamps, its engine enlarged to 4 litres, and, later, the novel option of a five-speed gearbox. Other improvements included electrically operated windows and standard front disc brakes. While it was a gentle evolution from the DB4, it was destined for mythical status when Eon Productions chose it for a starring role laden with special effects in the 1964 James Bond film *Goldfinger*. By the next show it was Bond's Aston for good.

By 1963, coachbuilder Harold Radford had diversified into mainstream cars. From right: his successful Mini Cooper, a luxury-trimmed Vauxhall Cresta and Rolls-Royce Silver Cloud. On the far left is a unique Ford Cortina coupé, the 'dream car' of Stirling Moss. (Vauxhall Heritage)

German carmaker NSU claimed a first, exhibiting the Spyder, a smart two-seater convertible styled by Bertone and the first mass-produced car with a Wankel rotary engine. In simple terms, a rotary engine is a shaft in a horizontal casing onto which a rotor is mounted (which looks triangular in profile) and rotates at high speed. The side injection of fuel and air is ignited into the spaces between each of the two tips of the triangle and the casing as they pass. It has no pistons or valves, weighs a lot less than a conventional engine, is more compact and very smooth. It was patented in 1929 by Dr Felix Wankel, hence the name. The Spyder had a single-rotor engine equivalent to only 498cc but was good for a claimed 100mph.

1964

The big BMC news for Earls Court 1964 was the grand Austin 1800. By now the company was making maximum publicity for the Mini's transverse engine and front-wheel-drive concept, and the 1800 was the largest recipient of the package. Although it looked ungainly, it offered a huge amount of passenger and luggage space in less than 14ft. It was meant to replace the 'Farina' saloons but was more expensive (£768 to £722 for a Cambridge) and BMC opted to keep the older design going. It was selling well but BMC's strategy of adding more and more cars to its range without paring away older models (the Morris Minor was still going) was to prove to be a mistake.

Reliant properly entered the sports coupé market with the Scimitar GT, replacing the short-lived Sabre of 1961. Also bodied in fibreglass with a six-cylinder Ford engine, it had been attractively styled by Ogle based on a design for the discontinued Daimler SP250.

Reliant's three-wheeler rival, Bond, had also branched into four-wheeled cars in 1963, with the Bond Equipe, a fibreglass coupé built on a Triumph Herald chassis, and retaining its doors.

Elva had been a respected kit-car manufacturer since the 1950s and surprised the show with the striking Elva GT, just 40in high with a mid-mounted 185bhp BMW engine in an aluminium body by Fissore of Turin. Only the one was ever built and Elva went back to kits, the last cars being made in 1968.

Britain in the 1960s was loosening up, but the female voice was little heard in the hubbub of mid-1960s Earls Court. In 1964 women at the show fell into three categories: the 'dolly birds' who clambered around cars in various stages of undress for press day; visiting female rally drivers encouraged to look under bonnets on same day; and companions to male visitors. In its show review, *Motor* magazine gave two pages to renowned newspaper columnist Marjorie Proops and gradually women started to get a voice. MG Magnette driver Marj was not impressed in 1964, though:

> A two-hour trudge around the Motor Show confirmed my opinion that most car salesmen treat the female prospective customer with a kind of amused tolerance, a sort of let's humour-the-little-woman attitude which makes serious lady car-shoppers feel like bashing them over the head with a back axle.

As motoring historian Anders Ditlev Clausager observed in *Britain's Motor Industry: The First 100 Years*, the second half of the 1960s proved to be a marked contrast with the first.

The rate of truly new cars tailed off, major names started to struggle and the government became increasingly interventionist.

As a prelude to its takeover by Leyland, BMC wrongly continued to believe (encouraged by government) that bigger was better, expanding its ranges and swallowing up car body makers Fisher & Ludlow in 1963 and Pressed Steel in 1965. Rootes, struggling in the wake of the Hillman Imp failure, allowed Chrysler USA to buy into the company in 1964.

1965

The SMMT marked the 50th International Motor Show in 1965 by a 1903 replica stand and twelve veteran cars. The Rolls-Royce Silver Shadow was easily the most outstanding new car, replacing the Silver Cloud with a completely different style. Gone were the upright stance and the suggestion of separate wings for a squarely styled

A modern Rolls for a new age; the Rolls-Royce Silver Shadow of 1965 was the coolest cruise through the West End. (Rolls-Royce Enthusiasts' Club)

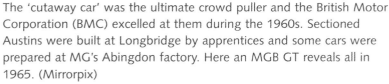

The 'cutaway car' was the ultimate crowd puller and the British Motor Corporation (BMC) excelled at them during the 1960s. Sectioned Austins were built at Longbridge by apprentices and some cars were prepared at MG's Abingdon factory. Here an MGB GT reveals all in 1965. (Mirrorpix)

Actor Peter Sellers was an obsessive car collector and regularly caused press day pandemonium while out shopping. Here he samples a Ferrari in 1965 with his then wife, actress Britt Ekland. (Mirrorpix)

saloon with a lower version of the R-R radiator grille (no longer a real radiator) and only carrying over the previous car's 6.2-litre V8 engine. A hydraulic system built under Citroën patents provided self-levelling suspension and fed the brakes: four-wheel discs supplied by three circuits to retain braking should one fail. Inside were the usual wood, leather and electrically adjustable seats. A Bentley version, the T1, was launched at the same time.

The Shadow could be driven by a chauffeur or an owner-driver, or a super-executive perhaps. In October 1965, the price was £6,557; the T1 £6,496. For the head of state and traditionalists, the Rolls-Royce Phantom V continued, starting at £9,517. This was Rolls-Royce's first car with all-unitary construction. The bodyshells may have been made amidst more humdrum makes at Pressed Steel but they were still sent to Rolls-Royce at Crewe to be rubbed down by hand and carefully painted. There was a waiting list for of a year soon after launch, but Rolls-Royce refused to speed up the traditional production process. Although the Shadow was announced

in October 1965, deliveries were held up to spring 1966 because of supply problems from Pressed Steel. The first Shadow remained in production until 1977, much modified in detail.

The other all-new car of the show, and certainly a more attainable one, was the Triumph 1300, in looks a scaled-down version of the 2000 but more technically adventurous in having front-wheel drive, now established as a good thing by BMC and favoured by Triumph's engineers for interior space, although they opted to leave the enlarged Herald engine in a north–south axis. The 1300 lasted until 1970, when Triumph used its bodyshell as the basis of both the cheap rear-drive Toledo and with front-drive as the 1500, which was then replaced by the rear-drive Dolomite.

At stand 166, Ogle had teamed up with motor glassmaker Triplex to place an estate car body onto a Reliant Scimitar GT to create the Triplex Glazing Test Special (GTS). Its purpose was to demonstrate what could be done with automotive glass, with the roof above and behind the driver fitted with heat-absorbing green-tinted Sundym

THE JAPANESE CAR IN BRITAIN

Slowly, one by one, they came. In May 1965 Daihatsu became the first Japanese manufacturer to export to Britain with the 797cc Compagno Berlina, and the arrival of Hino and Toyota at the 1965 Motor Show was the start of a process that would reshape motor manufacturing across the world.

Hino had started assembling Renault 4CVs in 1953 and by the mid 1960s was joining a herd of fledgling Japanese carmakers in commissioning Italian stylists to clothe their cars' sound engineering, quality and equipment. The Hino Contessa 1300 saloon and coupé were listed as 'price on application', but stand 154 contained four Toyota Coronas (Toyota would absorb Hino in 1967), the importer gearing up to supply the 1500 saloon at the end of February 1966, at £777.

Daihatsu joined Toyota (for a year) in the 1966 show catalogue. In 1967 the Toyo Kogyo Co. Ltd – better known as Mazda – arrived with its 110S Wankel-engined sports car and sensible saloons. By 1967 Japan was the second largest producer of motor vehicles after the United States, which it was cutting a swathe through. In 1968 Datsun and Honda finished the Japanese suite of brands which would cause British carmakers so much angst in the next decade. Coming in ranges were at once conservative and innovative, Japanese cars were well built, reliable and well equipped (most came with a radio), which was all most car buyers wanted. The British establishment hostility was instant. 'Do not run away with the idea that because these cars come from far-away mysterious Japan they must be perfect; they are an essential "with-it" purchase,' carped *Motorsport* in December 1967 before visiting the new British importers of Honda, Toyota and Mazda.

The flood started slowly: a total of 4,291 Japanese cars was imported to Britain in 1970. British Leyland built 788,737 and had 38 per cent of the market. By 1976 Datsun was the top importer with 6.8 per cent of the British market; Fiat and Volkswagen were second and third.

Some of these buyers may have actively wanted to buy a British car but there were times in the 1970s when strikes made it hard to get one. Once they tried Japanese, few went back. British Leyland had not only pushed the door open by badly built cars and poor service but provided Japanese importers with new dealers, according to Tony Ball, now back at Leyland, because of dealer cull initiated by sales director Filmer Paradise:

'Sack 'em! They will fold up their tents and disappear into the night.' I remember the phrase. And so with an act of tremendous arrogance and marketing stupidity he was instrumental in sacking over three thousand of the dealers networking. Of course every dealer who got his notice didn't fold up his tent, he took off nationally with every foreign franchise.

TOYOTA CORONA

JAPAN'S MOST EXCITING NEW EXPORT
DOUBLE CHECKED
A HUNDRED TIMES

When you choose Toyota Corona you get one of the worlds most reliable cars. A hundred close and careful checks are made before it leaves the factory — and again before it is exported. You'll be seeing a lot more of this car on our roads. Note the neat Japanese Arrow line styling. Study the fine attention given to every detail and look at the special deep acrylic paintwork. Try a demonstration run and see how silently it cruises. Speeds (Up to 90 m.p.h.) from an efficient 1500 c.c. engine. Economical on fuel (Up to 35 m.p.g.)

Other exciting features include self adjusting brakes, alternator, electric screen washers, heater/demister, four seal beam head-lamps, carpets, reversing lamp etc. full specification overleaf.

£777 INCLUDING PUR. TAX

CORONA 1500 STATION WAGON £829 INCLUDING PUR. TAX

Sole UK Concessionaires MOTOR IMPORTS Co., 7, Gresham Road, London, S.W.9 RED. 2438

Toyota arrived in Britain in 1965 and this simple advert sums up why British buyers were to take to Japanese cars in droves. (Toyota)

Actress Diana Rigg tries not to slide off a Lotus Elan coupé at the 1965 show. As Mrs Emma Peel she drove a soft top through two series of *The Avengers*. (Mirrorpix)

safety glass. Years ahead of the feature being offered on regular cars, the laminated windscreen contained a heated element. Its most substantial pillar was a considerable roll bar above and behind the front seats. A fully working glass testbed, the GTS was still being loaned out for publicity some five years later, some said still looking better than the production car it inspired, the Reliant Scimitar GTE.

You'd only know by looking under the bonnet of the red CV-8 on Jensen's stand that the West Bromwich carmaker had laid claim to two major technical innovations. It was dubbed the FF saloon, because all of its wheels were driven by a Ferguson four-wheel-drive system and stopped by Dunlop's Maxaret anti-lock brakes. It was the first time any car in the world had been so equipped and decades ahead of mainstream adoption. A last-minute addition to the Jensen stand was

a new convertible which had been code-named 'Project 66' with the usual 4.5-litre Chrysler engine. It appeared a rather more attractive alternative to the CV-8; it was £1,285 cheaper and brought back the Interceptor name. In the same big-engined way, AC showed its new AC 427 convertible – essentially a Cobra under a new Italian suit

Running from 20 October to Saturday 30 October (closed on the 24th), attendance at the 1965 show broke all records at 660,257 visitors, and the venue must have been deeply uncomfortable. *Motor* had warned its readers to simply avoid Saturdays. The best chance of seeing some cars close up was likely to be a Monday evening during thick fog. Stuffing that many people into a confined space was now alleged to cause the 'Show cold'. The admission price was raised for the following year to keep numbers under control.

1966

Opening fire on the Government was a tradition at the annual SMMT Motor Show dinner and on 18 October 1966 at the Grosvenor House hotel, SMMT's president, Sir Patrick Hennessey of Ford, moaned that his entreaties for a stable home market and better roads had gone unanswered, as purchase tax had gone up by 10 per cent, excise duty on cars by 16 per cent and the hire-purchase down payment had increased from 25 to 40 per cent: 'What we are now experiencing is chaos, either by design or misjudgement.' At the show Mr Edward Heath, leader of the Conservative opposition, said that the strikes, short-time working and redundancies in the motor industry were a 'national tragedy' without, of course, being obliged to do anything about it.

But cheer up, there was a new Ford Cortina! Although the Mk I Cortina continued to sell well in 1966, its successor was ready for the October show. Based on the structure of its predecessor, the new-style Cortina boasted a 2in increase in front and rear shoulder room, greater legroom and a little more boot space. Engine and trim choices increased and a Lotus and estate versions were quick

Vauxhall's 1966 'experimental styling exercise', the XVR was the work of its Luton styling studio. It featured gullwing doors, pop-up headlights and all independent suspension. The dashboard styling, the company says, was used to test reaction to ideas for the later Firenza. (Vauxhall Heritage)

to arrive. Convertible carmaker Crayford's relationship with Ford was firmly established and a convertible was exhibited alongside the new saloon, with the conversion work having been carried out in secret in previous weeks.

The most direct, not to say copycat, Cortina challenger was the Rootes Group's 1.7-litre Hillman Hunter and Singer Vogue, the first in its 'Arrow' series replacing all its Minx-derived cars. With its Cortina-style MacPherson-strut front suspension (a first for Rootes) and a light, strong bodyshell manufactured by Pressed Steel Fisher, it was a whole cubic weight lighter than its predecessor.

The 1.5-litre Minx followed in January 1967 and Rootes got busy badge-engineering Hillman, Humber, Singer and Sunbeam saloons and estates, plus the Rapier/Alpine coupé. Healthy sales followed but not enough to save Rootes from a full takeover by Chrysler US in 1967. With money fast running out, the Arrow cars were only allowed mild facelifts and sales tailed off as two further Cortina evolutions passed it by before ending production in 1979.

Jensen's styling went from oddball to handsome with the 1966 Interceptor, seen here in four-wheel-drive FF guise, denoted by twin vents in the front wings. (Jensen)

Aston Martin was signalling that it was looking for a new style with the two-seater DBS, styled by its preferred styling house, Touring of Milan. Although well received, the 1966 DBS was to be an automotive red herring.

The Jensen range had undergone a radical transformation: the CV-8 was gone, along with the Interceptor of 1965. After only two cars had been built, the show convertible and a later hardtop, Jensen had undergone a management change and taken a trip to Italy. The Interceptor name was now applied to a steel-bodied coupé with a novel glass tailgate, styled by Touring and initially built by Vignale. More brutal than an Aston Martin, the 1966 Interceptor was the ultimate Anglo-American GT, laden with equipment such as electric windows, power door locks, air conditioning and an automatic gearbox only. The Interceptor was £3,743, the more complex FF £5,340, which was recognisable by its twin air vents behind the front wheels. If you were a tycoon in the 1960s you had to swish up to meetings in an Interceptor. In fact, the 1969 Interceptor Director could be your mobile office, with back-seat space taken up by a console with a typewriter, radiotelephone and portable television.

The 1967 Jaguar Pirana, built by Bertone at the behest of the *Daily Telegraph*. The specification included an advanced air-conditioning system for cruising at 100mph with the windows closed. (LAT)

1967

By 1967 the British motorist was feeling truly put upon. An experimental 70mph speed limit had been introduced two years' earlier and was now permanent, and, although from the dawn of motoring you couldn't drive a car drunk, 1967 ushered in the first UK maximum legal drink drive limit and Transport Minister Barbara Castle introduced the breathalyser as a means of scientifically testing it. This formed the cheeky theme of this year's Pathé Motor Show film of cars which were easy enough for wifey to drive drunk hubby back from the pub, sprawled fatly in the reclining front seat.

Throughout the 1960s, Vauxhall had replaced or restyled its Victor range at great pace and in 1967 came the third series since 1961. The 'FD' Vauxhall Victor was bigger than its predecessors with pronounced 'Coke bottle' styling and all-new 1.6- and 2.0-litre rubber belt-driven single overhead cam engines, a first for a British car and considered very advanced for its time when other carmakers feared such things would snap. This Victor would be a major

In 1967 Chrysler USA had taken full ownership of Rootes. Chrysler Australia fielded its new Valiant and industry observers anticipated that it would be a replacement for the Humber Super Snipe. (Rootes, courtesy of Coventry History Centre)

The 1967 Lamborghini stand needed little adornment when it offered a glimpse of the Miura (right) and the Marzal (seen from behind, left). The Marzal was a 'concept car' before the term was coined, foreshadowing the Espada. (Mirrorpix)

influence on the third Cortina and its engine would form the basis of the next generation of Lotus cars.

Suddenly Rover's sedate ministerial car, the P5, had become a hot-rod with an American 3.5-litre V8 engine. The unit had famously started life in 1961 as a General Motors design for Buick, Pontiac and Oldsmobile models. It was a conventional V8 but highly unusual being cast in aluminium, and it was discarded by General Motors just two years later due to production and service defects (it required owners to use a specific type of antifreeze) but above all because it cost too much to build. However, it had gained a reputation for being highly tunable, and while shopping for a V8, Rover snapped up the manufacturing rights and used it to power Rover cars and Land Rovers for decades, only going out of production in 2004. Specialist car makers also latched onto it: Morgan from 1968, then Marcos but TVR would make best use of it right into the 2000s.

BMC had become British Motor Holdings in 1966 after buying Jaguar (at the invitation of Jaguar's Sir William Lyons), though it was not a prosperous combining. Mismanaged and failing to reap

financial rewards from its front-wheel-drive cars, in 1966–67 BMH made a loss after tax of nearly £4 million. In 1967 its newest cars were the Austin 3-Litre, a front-engined rear-drive car based on the centre section of the 1800, and the MGC, a six-cylinder version of the B, neither of which the market wanted. While Ford and Vauxhall regularly restyled and re-engineered their cars, the former BMC management had believed the Issigonis formula so advanced that it could let its front-drivers go on with only detail changes. The biggest news for 1967 was that the 1100 had become a 1300.

The Aston Martin DBS of 1966 had become something quite different for 1967. Having created two prototypes, Touring had gone out of business and Aston had hastily gone to its in-house designer William Towns, at the time working on seats, to style the new car. It would be such as success that Towns would become the country's best-known car designer of the 1970s.

The new DBS had been unveiled on 25 September 1967 at Blenheim Palace, Oxfordshire, at that stage intending to supplement it with the DB6 (last of the DB4/5 line). Priced at £5,500 it was a real dream car. With the full-width four-headlamp grille it was a determined break with the previous style and would take Aston Martin into the 1980s. A V8 engine was late into production so it was launched with the same 4.0-litre engine as the DB6. The rear suspension was a more sophisticated De Dion axle. In a new heavier bodyshell the engine gave the DBS a reputation for being relatively slow, although a 145mph max speed was claimed until the V8 arrived in 1969.

New Aston or not, it was impossible to ignore Lamborghini at the 1967 show. Founded in 1963 by successful tractor builder Ferruccio Lamborghini, it was now seriously worrying Ferrari, even though it didn't have a racing programme. The P400 Miura had stolen the November 1965 Turin show with its V12 engine both being mid (behind the seats and ahead of the axle) and transversely mounted wrapped in a stunning shape by Marcello Gandini at Bertone.

In addition to the Miura, the Lamborghini stand was a magnet for the cameras on press day 1967 thanks to the £11,000 Marzal prototype named after a strain of fighting bull. A long, low projectile also styled by Bertone, it had gullwing doors giving access to four seats. It was a prelude to the front-engined V12 Espada, which appeared the following year with two conventional doors.

The carriagework section of the ground floor had long seen the departure of the old British coachbuilders, their place taken

The Beatles loved their cars. Here in 1967 John Lennon examines an Iso Rivolta S4, an Italian four-door supercar with a Corvette engine, which he bought on the spot for £8,000 and had delivered the following January. (Mirrorpix)

by the Italians, who the world's carmakers were running to for off-the-peg style.

Also from Bertone came the Jaguar Pirana coupé. It had been built on the orders of the editor of the *Daily Telegraph* Friday colour magazine, John Anstey. In the mid 1960s the *Telegraph* had the money and the ambition to make a name for itself in the motoring world (its yearly Motor Show guide was a big seller). Reportedly enthused by a chat with Nuccio Bertone at the March 1967 Geneva show, Anstey asked a group of motoring journalists what features would make up their ideal grand touring car and persuaded his bosses to part with £20,000. Sir William Lyons of Jaguar sold the *Telegraph* the chassis and running gear of a Jaguar E-Type 2+2, which was widened to take new bodywork in steel and aluminium by Bertone in Turin between April and October 1967.

The handsome end result was meant to showcase British automotive companies, so Smiths Industries donated the instruments and developed a bespoke air conditioning system and Phillips the very new in-car cassette player/recorder. Connolly trimmed the leather seats, Triplex provided the Sundym glass and Britax the safety belts, with flashing dashboard lights telling the occupants to use them.

The Pirana was just the start of several years of the magazine's involvement in British car styling and author Giles Chapman fully detailed the competition in *Classic & Sportscar* 1988. At a time when even British-owned companies headed to Italy for their car styling, Anstey tried to fly the flag for domestic car design into the 1970s.

Last from Italy, Ercole Spada of Zagato had rebodied a Rover 2000 TC as a four-seater coupé, the TCZ. It was seen attracting the interest of several Rover executives at the show, but was never taken up as a production design, Rover having its own problems as it merged with Leyland and a prototype Alvis coupé had been shelved.

If a second-hand car wouldn't do and your family was too big for a Mini or Ford Anglia, in the 1960s and '70s countries of the Soviet Union would sell you something bigger at an artificially low price, in exchange for much-needed foreign currency. Czechoslovakia's rear-engined Skoda 1000MB and even Wartburg's 353 Knight, from Eisenach in East Germany, had their fans. Desperately cheap and desperately crude, its three-cylinder two-stroke engine trailed a cloud of smoke behind it as oil had to be added to the petrol mixture.

Tested by *Autocar* in 1967, Russia's Moskvitch de Luxe appeared a smart new car but was described as 'backward'. Yet it was built like a tank, had a starting handle in its big toolkit (which many buyers missed) and cost £647 in the UK when Russian buyers queued to pay £1,900. The 1968 *Daily Express Motor Show Review* seemed outraged just to be listing it: 'Communist University dons and trades union bosses, hoping for a place in some future Russian puppet Government of Britain, may make ritual obeisance here, but even they are unlikely to buy until the creaking Russian industry is brought up to date with factories built by Western capitalism.'

The 1967 Vauxhall Victor caught Ford on the hop with up-to-date styling, which others followed, and a more advanced engine, but it didn't outsell the Cortina. (Vauxhall Heritage)

There was much excitement over Honda's mini car, the N360, aimed directly at the original Mini. It had technical and price interest. A 354cc two-cylinder air-cooled engine came from Honda's motorcycle background, drove the front wheels and it was priced £50 lower than the equivalent Mini. *Motorsport* magazine shouted at its readers to leave it alone: 'Are we going to let it stamp into the ground our water-cooled 4-cylinder f.w.d Mini with its more sophisticated suspension and its great international rally successes? Well, are we?'

The most technically interesting car of the show had to be NSU Ro80, a roomy front-drive aerodynamic saloon with styling by Claus Luthe that was years ahead of its time. The Ro stood for Rotary engine, a twin-rotor Wankel design of only 995cc but which gave 115bhp, enough for 100mph autobahn cruising. A semi-automatic transmission disengaged the clutch by finger pressure on the gear lever. An instant Car of the Year, it was hoped that the high UK price of £1,978 would fall as sales got going, but by 1968 it was £2,232. The motor industry was to have a torrid love affair with the smooth and compact rotary engine up until the early 1970s, when unreliability and high fuel consumption would kill it off.

Mazda exhibited the second rotary-engine car of the show, a single Sport Cosmo 110S developing 108bhp, the equivalent power of a 2-litre engine from its total 982cc. It was priced at an eye-watering £2,607 with tax but only two were ever said to be sold in the UK. Its presence was more useful for attracting new dealers to sign up.

TVR Engineering was a new name for the 1967 show guide. Having been in precarious business since 1947 as a small-scale sports car maker, its reputation was growing in the 1960s, especially in America. A Tuscan V8 (the new name for the Griffith), Cortina-engined Vixen and the dainty TVR Tina occupied stand 138.

Styled by Brit Trevor Fiore (formerly Frost), the Tina was new TVR boss Martin Lilley's idea for sales in a different, less macho, part of the market after the Fiat 850 Spyder. Based on a Hillman Imp and bodied by Fissore in Italy, a Tina convertible had appeared at Geneva 1966. Both convertible and coupé Tina were at Earls Court 1967. Billed at a likely £998, they caused a stir. But in its then shaky financial state, TVR was in no position to volume build a steel-bodied car. The obvious option was to try to contract the work out. Abortive talks were held with Rootes, Jensen and even Aston Martin to build under licence until the plug was pulled.

Mergers now seemed the only way for British carmakers to survive and in 1968 came the big one, bringing a name which would dominate the news in the next decade: the British Leyland Motor Corporation.

The starting point had been Leyland Commercial Vehicles buying Standard Triumph in 1960 and Rover in 1967. British Motor Holdings Ltd (BMH) was in a parlous state. As detailed in Graham Turner's *The Leyland Papers* Prime Minister Harold Wilson invited both Sir Donald Stokes of Leyland and Sir George Harriman of BMH to dinner at Chequers in October, pushing a process which had already started in the national interest. What had been a merger became a takeover of a weaker company by a stronger one, and British Leyland was announced in January 1968, effective at the end of May with Stokes in charge.

The £500 million merger between Leyland and BMH (although it continued to use the BMC name) created the second largest motor manufacturer in Europe after Volkswagen and its twenty-nine factories across the UK made everything from steamrollers to sports cars. That would prove to be exactly the problem. In 1968, though, it was greeted with optimism.

1968

New Leyland logo on its stand or not, in 1968 Earls Court once more belonged to Jaguar with the XJ6. Developed over four years at a cost of £6 million, it swept away the Mk II and S-Type with a choice of 2.8- and 4.2-litre six-cylinder XJ engines. It astonished the public with its soundproofing, superlative ride and comfort, and was compared to the Rolls-Royce Silver Shadow. Dunlop had even developed a new kind of tyre for it. Yet again, though, Jaguar produced this for the reasonable starting price of £1,797 tax paid. There was an immediate waiting list. When, in 1972, it was given Jaguar's new V12 engine it became even more desirable.

   Little Reliant had pulled off a real coup with the launch of the Scimitar GTE. Taking inspiration from the Triplex GTS estate of

Reliant invented a new kind of car with the Scimitar GTE – the sports estate. By 1971 it was enjoying royal patronage. (Giles Chapman Picture Library)

The August 1968 Soviet Trade Exhibition was the target of marchers from Trafalgar Square protesting at the Soviet invasion of Czechoslovakia. (Mirrorpix)

Four Earls Court cleaning ladies remove smudgy fingerprints from a BMC 1800 at the 1968 show. (Mirrorpix)

1965, the Scimitar had been restyled by Tom Karen of Ogle with an estate-style body rear of the front doors ending with a lift-up glass tailgate. 'Scimitar GT/E Join the GT/E set!' said the advertising, and Reliant could genuinely claim that it had combined a grand tourer and capacious estate in one car, including rear-seat backrests which split and folded forward individually. Underneath it was still a Ford 2.5- or 3.0-litre V6 engine in a separate chassis. It became a terribly smart car to have, even smarter after Princess Anne became an owner in 1970. The glass-tailgated sports estate became a much-copied type in the 1970s.

As far as big show debuts go, that was about it for 1968. British Leyland was preparing its new wave and Ford had ignored the tradition of launching near to the British Motor Show and replaced the Anglia with the Anglo-German Escort in January 1968, with UK production at Halewood, near Liverpool, and Genk, Belgium. It was an instant hit across Europe.

The days of the big crush were over. When the doors closed in 1968 it transpired there had been a 27 per cent drop in attendance compared with 1967: 444,291 from 607,402. Overseas visitors were down by 10,000.

1969

When it came to dividing up the floor space for 1969, British Leyland was likely to be able to call the shots because it would have individual stands for all its brands. 'Collectively the British Motor Corporation, British Motor Holdings, had tremendous influence in requiring space within Earls Court, and within reason always got it,' recalls Tony Ball, having departed BMC sales and marketing in 1967. 'As you came into the hall the first one almost on the left was the key position. Everybody liked to be there, and to some degree you had to compromise year by year.'

Lord Stokes had begun to rationalise his empire. The Austin-Healey and Riley names had gone and, more grievously to enthusiasts, so had the Mini Cooper. There was a new kind of Mini, the Clubman, and, given that the Mini had been largely undeveloped for ten years, this was big news. The Clubman saloon and estate had a new front which made it look like a Ford Cortina (the stylist Roy Haynes had indeed styled the Mk II Cortina), and Barker and Horner called it the 'Cyrano de Bergerac Mini'. Inside was a new dashboard with face level air vents, new seats and, at long last, wind-up windows. The top non-Cooper Clubman was the 1275GT with 59bhp. More pleasing to the accountants, the Clubman was £130 more than the old-nosed Mini, which carried on in the smaller engine ranges.

The first all-new Leyland car, the Austin Maxi, had been launched in April 1969 and was clearly a problem child. On paper it was pioneering, a five-door 1500cc family hatchback in the mould of the 1965 Renault 16 but benefitting from the Issigonis transverse engine layout for even more interior space. The engine was a new overhead cam unit built at a £16 million new engine plant at Cofton Hackett, and it was the first British family car with a five-speed gearbox. Unveiled to the press in Estoril, Portugal, the Maxi had a dreadful cable-operated gear change, which sometimes made it hard to select any gear at all. Leyland introduced the much-improved Maxi

1750 at the 1970 show, with a rod-operated gear change and new dashboard. Whilst not selling in the optimistic volumes predicted, it remained well liked by enough British buyers until 1981.

With hindsight there was a hint of the new look for Leyland cars of the 1970s at Earls Court 1969. On its bodymaker Pressed Steel Fisher's stand was the Zanda, a bright green wedge-shaped design for a mid-engined sports car with a Maxi engine, illustrating the abilities of the Pressed Steel styling department's computer-aided design.

Barker and Horner were dismissive, but the 'wedge' was to dominate 1970s sports car styling. As to the Zanda, its stylist Harris Mann would apply its 'wedginess' to Leyland cars through the following decade to notable effect.

Launched the previous January, the 1969 Ford Capri coupé was already an object of desire for many motorists and schoolboys. Only just available for Earls Court, the range-topping Capri 3000GT boasted a 3-litre V6 engine. Crayford was showing a convertible Capri and its new amphibious Amphicat, which would take up a good part of its business in the 1970s.

Looking like it had escaped from a science-fiction film, most outrageous car of the 1969 show was the Adams brothers' Probe 16, designed by former Marcos designers Dennis and Peter Adams and this year's *Daily Telegraph* magazine-backed car on the Institute of British Carriage and Automobile Manufacturers (IBCAM) stand. A mid-engined two-seater with an Austin 1800 engine, at 86cm high it was so low you had to enter through the roof. Dennis Adams explained it as 'just a private fancy, to get something as low as possible and doing whatever was necessary to achieve it'. Unlike the other IBCAM/*Telegraph* cars, the Probe 16 went into small-scale production and was featured in the 1971 film *A Clockwork Orange*.

5 UNCERTAINTY
1970–76

The Range Rover and the Triumph Stag were striking 1970 show entries for the two-and-a-half-year-old British Leyland, Ford brought out an all-new Cortina and the Bond Bug was an orange slice of fun. Rather than a Royal, the SMMT even invited England football team captain Bobby Moore CBE to open the show. It was a great start to a decade which has a fair claim to be the most miserable in British motoring history, beset by strikes and marauding imports.

The Range Rover was something completely new, a high-riding two-door estate with the four-wheel-drive capabilities of a permanently engaged Land Rover, the smooth and powerful Rover V8 engine and an interior smart enough to rival prestige saloons (although these first RRs did have hose-down rubber flooring). *Autocar*'s critics at the show, Barker and Horner, by now sounding somewhat jaundiced in their copy, predicted the Range Rover's future: 'Already one can expect demand for the Range Rover far outstripping output; many of us expect it to be an "in" vehicle even for those in no need of its very special qualities.'

It hadn't always been easy getting a Land Rover shown at Earls Court, recalls John Baumber, about to become a new vehicle development engineer for the later Rover SD1:

Land Rover and Range Rover were not looked on as 'cars' and we had to battle to get them on the stands. Vehicles were specially prepared and the 'hidden' parts – under bonnet, undertrays, door shuts etc. –

Norwegian actress Julie Ege waits for directions while a man probes the build quality of the new 1970 Ford Cortina. (Ford Motor Company Ltd)

that were not painted in production were all specially finished and bore little resemblance to the production model. Not allowed now!

The Triumph Stag promised as much as the Range Rover but famously failed. In the late 1960s Triumph had asked Michelotti to create a four-seat convertible from its 2000 saloon and this became the Stag, fitted with a 145bhp 3-litre engine of Triumph's own design. The handsome convertible with a built-in roll bar was intended to take on Mercedes-Benz and was initially in high demand but sadly the engine had built-in design faults which meant the car acquired an early reputation for overheating which depressed sales for the rest of its run to 1977.

Although the Ford Escort and Capri had been launched outside of show season, Ford managed to keep its third Cortina under wraps until Earls Court 1970. But this was not just a new Ford Cortina, this was an all-new Ford Cortina: new styling, new floorpan, new engines and new suspension. Critics were keen to point out that its curved 'Coke bottle' styling resembled the 1967 Vauxhall Victor (still on sale), a look which Vauxhall seemed to have discarded for its new square-lined 1970 Viva.

Ford was successfully rationalising both European and American production; the Cortina shared much with the new German Taunus launched the same year, and Ford of America's new Beetle-basher, the latterly notorious Pinto hatchback, was at Earls Court, sharing an engine with the Cortina.

Also completely new, the Hillman Avenger took pride of place on the Rootes/Chrysler stand. It was a much-needed conventionally engineered car to slot into the market below the 'Arrow' Hunter-based cars with 1248 and 1498cc engines driving the rear wheels. Available in two- or four-door saloon form or as a five-door estate, an Avenger was a viable alternative to a lower-price Ford Cortina, an Escort or a Vauxhall Viva.

Bond – under Reliant's ownership – sneaked its Bug past the three-wheeler ban by sticking two together. (LAT)

The 1970 Volkswagen boys did not go down well in place of the 'dollies', despite the tight trousers. (LAT)

Vauxhall's 1970 SRV followed the Italian fashion for very low pointy cars. (Vauxhall Heritage)

A revolution was going on at the 1970 Volkswagen stand: firstly a new saloon car with front-wheel drive and a water-cooled engine, rather than rear and air cooled, the K70. It was the first fruit of Audi-NSU, formed by the merger with Auto Union. NSU had been set to launch the K70 at the March 1969 Geneva Motor Show but Volkswagen withdrew it shortly before the merger that month, re-engineered it to suit its manufacturing techniques and launched it with its own badge at the September 1970 Paris Motor Show. In the UK the K70 was considered interesting but too expensive, and its economics were disastrous, said to share not a single nut and bolt with another Volkswagen. The Passat sounded its death knell in 1973.

The second surprise from Volkswagen was a complete lack of 'dolly birds' perched on bonnets for the photographers and dawdling workmen. The press was fascinated to see instead three men, referred to as 'male models', in white trousers with orange shirts and white ties, ready to answer questions about the product. 'This year there will be no girls,' said Mr Alan Dix, managing director of Volkswagen Motors. 'I do not think that you sell any more Volkswagens by filling the boot with buxom, semi-clothed girls.'. The *Daily Mirror* did a boobs and bums picture special, with a picture of a 1969 Volkswagen girl as it wondered 'was this the last of the VW dollies?' Mr Dix also caused controversy by denigrating the show, saying Earls Court was dusty and dirty, that most of his staff went down with colds or sore throats and that he'd be happy if VW only had to attend every other

year. The SMMT came back with, 'We and the half a million people who visit the show do not agree with Mr Dix.'

Having only offered the DS and the Citroën Ami and Dyane in the UK through the 1960s (the latter cars based on the 2CV, which itself was still thought not worth importing), Citroën provided technical fascination with the aerodynamic GS saloon, with hydro-pneumatic suspension and a horizontally opposed 1.0-litre air-cooled engine. Pundits ruefully observed that it strongly resembled the Pininfarina aerodynamic saloons which BMC hadn't dared put into production. Mobbed by crowds even at press days, the GS was correctly tipped to be the Car of the Year for 1970.

At the other extreme of the price range, Citroën's SM coupé had taken the Paris show by storm, the culmination of a co-operation between the French company and Maserati agreed in 1968. The most expensive and fastest Citroën to that date, it combined all the hydro-pneumatic tricks of the DS into a beautiful three-door with a Maserati-derived 2.7-litre V6 engine driving the front wheels.

The SM was never produced in right-hand-drive form and only 327 were imported out of a 13,000 run to 1975. Also to be seldom seen in the UK, Alfa Romeo showed its new flagship coupé, the Bertone-styled V8 Montreal.

it was not a bad year for very small British car manufacturers. Produced in Wales, the Gilburn Invader estate took on the idea of the Reliant Scimitar GT/E and was also based around a Ford V6 engine, while the Ginetta G21 was a smart new sports car also with Ford power. Marcos of Wiltshire replaced its curvy sports coupé of the 1960s with the odd-looking Mantis and folded the following year (although subsequently revived).

Of the small car makers though, Reliant managed to grab a great deal of attention again with a six-wheeled Bond Bug, two three-wheelers joined at the rear. Being classed as motorcycles for licensing purposes, regular three-wheelers weren't allowed at the Motor Show.

Reliant had taken over Bond, its rival producer of three-wheelers in 1969 and the bug, an orange-shaped wedge with a swing-open canopy was an attempt to inject some fun into the sedate and small market for three-wheelers. Styled by Tom Karen of Ogle and based on the Reliant Regal chassis, a 700cc engine sat behind the front wheel giving all of 29bhp. The Bug was marketed as a wacky alternative to a Mini, a Hillman Imp or a Fiat 850 and for a while

Shots from the 1970 show. Above, the AC 428 was the last of the Cobra line with a bonnet to be sprawled over. Right, cabaret singer Patsy Snell (on the left) professed surprise when a photographer asked her to show a bit more flesh. (Author's collection)

was a real attention grabber, but demand fizzled out after a couple of years. Reliant carried on alone in the three-wheeler market with the 1973 Robin.

While a new Viva took care of day-to-day business, Vauxhall's styling studio drew crowds to its stand with the Special Research Vehicle (SRV), a four-seat concept car which could have easily emerged from an Italian styling house. The sharp, pointed projectile was 16ft 8in long but stood only 41½in high. Engineers as well as stylists had spent a great amount of time on it. It had a mocked-up turbo-charged transverse engine in the rear based on a Victor unit, instruments which swung out with the opening doors, an aerofoil, electric self-levelling suspension and a 'manometer' to measure air pressure on the car's hull. It still survives at Luton in Vauxhall's heritage collection.

There had been a change of management at the SMMT in 1970. 'SMMT President, Douglas Richards, explains that the object of the show is to be exciting,' said *Motor*, 24 October 1970, ready to defend Earls Court: 'You may be able to see more examples of various makes in the Continental exhibitions spread over far too many acres, but not everybody who goes to a racecourse wants to get all that close to the horses. It is an "occasion" and the Motor Show is very much the same.'

Much was expected from new exhibitions manager Gerry Kunz, the son of well-known pianist and entertainer Charlie Kunz. Gerry died in 2011, acknowledged in his obituary as the architect and brains behind the success of the Motor Show, Commercial Motor Show and the Smithfield Livestock Show. He was awarded the OBE for services to agriculture.

Kunz made his mark straight away, allowing BMW to march a burly Bavarian band through Earls Court and to play on its stand, much to the ire of other exhibitors. Despite their protests, he presciently realised that the event would attract widespread press attention and TV coverage, which it did before he prudently shut it down. His word was to become Motor Show law.

1971

The following year was one of those where little at the show was truly new, at least as far as the motoring press were concerned. But it was a chance to see the new Morris Marina, British Leyland's utterly conventional rear-wheel-drive saloon and belated attempt take on the Cortina, Escort and the Hillman Avenger, presented to the press in Cannes earlier in the year.

Swiftly under way after the 1968 Leyland/BMH merger, the specification of the Marina was dictated by the corporate parts bin. The front suspension was of similar design to the Morris Minor, the gearbox from the new rear-driven Triumph Toledo and 1500, and the engines from the trusty 1.3-litre A Series and 1.8-litre B Series (with twin carburettors for the performance versions).

Styled by Roy Haynes, poached from Ford having styled the Mk II Cortina, the Marina was notable in having its two-door version as a coupé style, and Haynes managed to do this at little extra cost by retaining the saloon's front doors. It did prove to be a true marketing point. It was hoped that the Marina would have been ready for the 1970 London Motor Show, where it would have faced the new Cortina, but its frantic timing meant it had to wait another year, by which time the Cortina and Escort had gained yet more ground. Total project time was thirty-five months.

After a well-documented handling embarrassment in which *Autocar's* discovery of the early Marinas' propensity for potentially lethal understeering required the front suspension to be modified before sale, the Marina range gained an estate version and settled down to a UK sales career which peaked at 115,000 in 1973.

The naked press-day antics of Susan and Helen (see p.93) and, for some unexplained reason, a chimpanzee, drew a lot of attention to the new TVR M Series and the TVR SM prototype. Although not credited at the time, British Leyland stylist Harris Mann had been commissioned to produce an all-new TVR shape. Bearing no resemblance to past TVRs, its upswept rear tailgate and pop-up headlamps were echoed in the later Lotus Elite. At the show the SM was said to be scheduled for production, adding to the existing TVR range and fitted with the fuel-injected Triumph six-cylinder engine, selling for the price of a fully built Lotus Elan +2 (around £2,500). Yet again like the Tina, the company was unable to put it into production because nothing had been done in terms of any car design and you couldn't actually see out of the rear window.

With a dearth of significant production cars, one-offs like the SM at least provided a novelty for paying visitors. There was barely a trace of the British coachbuilders now.

After the science-fiction Adams' Probe of 1969, and the not dissimilar Marcos XP of 1970 (an ex-Le Mans car), this year's *Daily Telegraph*/IBCAM British styling exercise was a little less outlandish, but not much. The Siva was a gullwinged two-seater in a fashionable wedge shape, possessing a rear-mounted Aston Martin V8. It was commissioned from Siva, a company owned by Neville Trickett, best

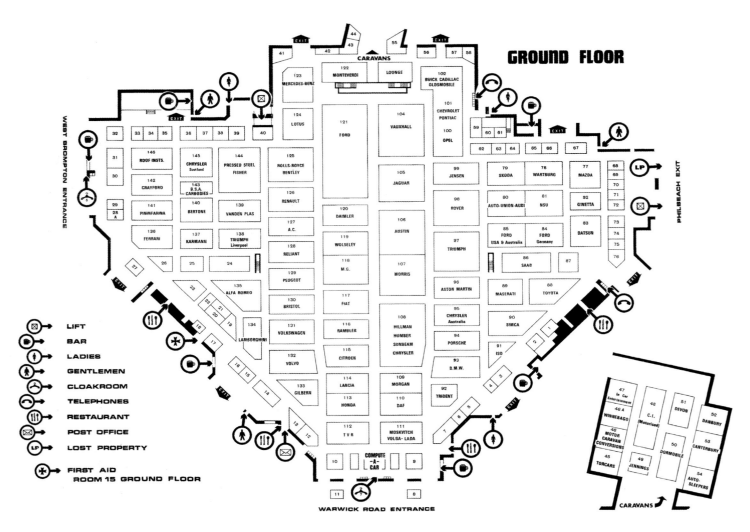

This 1971 ground-floor plan contains many now-vanished names. The central block is dominated by British Leyland brands but TVR has managed to be first past the turnstiles. (SMMT, courtesy of Coventry History Centre)

known for creating hot-rods and the mini sprint. *Car* magazine called it a 'mess' with no luggage space, crash protection or rear visibility and said the *Telegraph* should have paid him to call in a professional designer rather than 'allowing an embarrassed world to think this is the best Britain can do'.

Similar scorn was reserved for Skoda, which was showing the S110 GT coupé from Prague University, with a cut-off tail featuring sixteen circles for its various lamps. Access was via a single forward-hinged canopy like the Bond Bug, and it did at least have room for luggage and a spare wheel.

A replica Moon Buggy on the General Motors Stand completed the mix of show oddities. 'The SMMT used to be pretty snotty nosed about allowing in exhibits that weren't intended for production and purchase,' said *Car*'s reviewer. 'Now I'm beginning to wonder if they weren't being wondrous wise.'

Thirty-four years old in 1971, the Earls Court exhibition centre had had its share of management changes but had settled into a comfortable co-existence with Olympia, retaining big names such as the Crufts dog show, Boat Show and the Ideal Home Exhibition.

But London's tenure of the Motor Show was not guaranteed. All the London exhibition halls had keen competition from Birmingham venues which were closer to the industrial centres of the Midlands and invariably cheaper. The idea of a National Exhibition Centre had begun in 1969, a contest between Northolt in West London and a site near Elmdon airfield, Birmingham. While the government of the day favoured Birmingham, it stopped short of owning or funding show spaces, so a new one would need full commercial backing and big name shows – like the Motor Show – to be viable.

Compared with the bright optimism and multiple debuts of interesting cars in the first half of the 1960s, there was a weary cynicism to the car magazine's show reports of the new decade. Encouraged by the prospect of a venue other than Earls Court, Jeff Daniels in *Autocar*'s 1971 post-show number asked whether we needed a Motor Show at all, rightly pointing out that since that first Crystal Palace exhibition it had been essentially a trade fair to which the organisers saw an advantage in charging the public to come in. It was not, after all, possible to buy a car at the show.

Fewer car launches – and those only by British-based manufacturers – were tied to the Earls Court show. With four-year product cycles, fewer manufacturers were able to, or wanted to launch at a relatively small show and try and compete with a lot of other noise. One of

the year's most interesting new cars, the Alfa Romeo Alfasud was launched at the 1971 Turin show the month after Earls Court.

Annual visitor numbers were respectable but Daniels, as others were doing, questioned the need for there to be a British Motor Show every year when Berlin had been dropped in favour of a greatly expanded bi-annual Frankfurt show in 1951, covering fourteen halls. Even though Paris had posted over a million visitors in 1968 there was talk of 1971 being its last annual show. The expense of exhibiting was a problem for car makers having to invest to keep up with safety and pollution regulations whilst contending with industrial action – Parisian traffic was paralysed by a Metro strike for 1971 at show time. It went bi-annual after 1976.

With the post-war motoring excitement long gone, was the Earls Court show all that interesting anyway? The cars never moved and visitors thronged to anything else that did, such as cutaway cars, but even these were in decline. And no more caravans please, *Autocar* pleaded. A small selection of trailer caravans would book free space year by year, and in 1971 they were absent with only motor caravans left. The Caravan Show was only eleven days later. How about a display of more exotica, such as Ferraris, Monteverdis and Lamborghinis?

But it was still a special day out, even if you worked in the industry, as John Baumber recalls:

> As an engineer, one had to justify the visit (expenses paid!) by researching a particular aspect of any new competitor vehicle. This was before the days of digital cameras so any unique feature (I remember one year of researching door check strap mechanisms) had to be done by sketches and noting the vehicle model for future reference. We didn't know it at the time but it was an early attempt at benchmarking!

On 12 November 1971 outline planning permission was given for Britain's first custom-built national exhibition centre to be developed on green belt land at Bickenhill, south of Birmingham. Final planning permission was conditional on the developers ensuring the centre blended in with the landscape.

Expected to be finished by 1975, the £14 million complex was to be run by Birmingham City Council and the Birmingham Chamber of Trade. It was to include 1 million sq.ft of exhibition halls, a 1,000-seat conference centre, shopping centre and a 500-bedroom hotel.

SHOWING IT ALL

Using scantily clad women to adorn cars was once a well-tried technique to get your car into the tabloids before the show opened to the public. Each decade of Earls Court press day photos reflected a society loosening until the clothes came off altogether. Custom car magazines of the 1970s were alternative soft-core porn.

In the 1940s and '50s nice young ladies in blouses and skirts opened the doors and boots and pretended to drive Earls Court cars. By 1960 the bikini was to be seen. It soon became standard wear along with more outlandish garments such as chainmail and leather.

The state of undress of the Motor Show 'dollies' was down to company policy. As you might have expected, family carmakers Vauxhall, British Leyland, Chrysler and Ford didn't do sexy. For a time in the 1960s Aston Martin got a bit leery, then calmed down. You could travel a few miles east to Soho and see far more flesh on show, but overexposure and cars seemed to attract much more comment. Models were hired for the day, came out for pictures and went home.

It was a ritual that the established car magazines were starting to mock or condemn by the early 1970s. Ralph Thoresby, writing his 'Private View' in *Motor*, October 1970, recounted TVR's creation of pandemonium: 'Helen Jones sat huddled in an ankle-length black cardigan, looking very young and very sad,' he wrote. She then flung her cardigan off to reveal a one-piece bikini. 'She squirmed this way and that, rarely smiled, didn't say a word, and appeared rather bewildered by it all. Then a TVR man flung her cardigan over to her over the heads of the photographers, she slipped back into it and crept back to the office.'

There was only one way to top this, or rather bottom it. Having already modelled nude for TVR in Blackpool, in 1971 Helen Jones and Susan Shaw proceeded to recreate the look on the show stand sprawled over the SM prototype. Such was the crush that the fence collapsed leaving a number of men with white stripes on their trousers as it had been newly painted. The posing had to be repeated. Officially boss Martin Lilley was not to know this would happen. 'The press release stuff was done the night before press day and there were just a few workmen around,' he told the author in 2008. 'On the day, the girls wore big long coats and just walked onto the stand, then took them off. But they were very discreet about it. The press loved it – I used to go Earls Court on the Tube and the next day there were people reading *The Mirror*, and all I could see was TVR.'

Topless bonnet adornment had a few more years' mileage, chiefly with TVR, but by the late 1970s the clothes were starting to go back on.

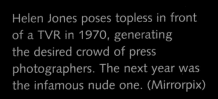

Helen Jones poses topless in front of a TVR in 1970, generating the desired crowd of press photographers. The next year was the infamous nude one. (Mirrorpix)

1972

For 1972 the Earls Court Motor Show was open on a Sunday for the first time, the presumed aim to boost attendance amid the talk that it should be bi-annual. Again it boasted few debuts but had a first glimpse of some important new cars. This was truly the year of the supermini: a new term to describe something slightly larger than a Mini with front-wheel drive and a hatchback. The Fiat 127 had started life the previous year with a separate bootlid but in 1972 sprouted a tailgate. It was joined by Renault's new 5, the first car to have moulded plastic grey bumpers which were part of the its styling.

From Honda came the Civic. This was the game-changer: well made, easy to drive with a refined 1.2-litre four-cylinder water-cooled engine and perfectly acceptable styling. It was a hit in Europe and the United States and, like the Fiat and Renault, sold in vast numbers. They all got a good lead in the supermini market, which others such as Ford and Vauxhall entered cautiously late and which British Leyland was continuously distracted from.

A new British name made its first Earls Court appearance: Panther, set to be a quirky and interesting addition to the 1970s British motoring scene. The firm was founded in Byfleet Surrey, in 1972, by Robert Jankel, who, having made his money in textiles, turned to cars. He'd always wanted a 1930s SS Jaguar but, when he found out how much they were, he became determined to build a near facsimile himself that was good enough to put into production as the Panther J72. A 1930s-style body clothed a tubular frame with a Jaguar XJ6 3.8-litre engine and disc brakes. In 1973 a J72 cost £5,285 and was joined by a V12 version at a heady £9,500 which would buy you a Ferrari Dino with change.

There was other British sports car news. Despite being lauded as one of the 'in' cars of the 1960s, the Jensen Interceptor had not been enough to stop the company lurching into crisis. Its staple income had come from assembling the Austin-Healey 3000 and the Sunbeam Tiger. In 1967 both cars were axed by their makers and Jensen's business was thrown into turmoil. Spurned by Leyland, Donald Healey himself teamed up with European car importer Kjell Qvale with a plan for a new Healey 3000. Healey joined the Jensen board and Qvale became majority shareholder in 1970.

The Jensen-Healey was launched at the 1972 Geneva show with a version of the new Lotus 507 2.0-litre engine before it had been proven in a Lotus, a rushed decision to get the car into production. As Colin Chapman's new engine was still in the development stage, he was unwilling to offer a comprehensive warranty. This was to cost Jensen dearly and the lack of engine development started to show after the Healey's 1972 launch. A flow of letters from Jensen to Lotus bemoaned carburettors which leaked petrol if the car was parked downhill, high oil consumption and under-bonnet fires. The car gained such a poor reputation that it never really shook off. Jensen was fatally hit by the fuel crisis with its gas-guzzling Interceptor and despite a modest upturn in Healey sales with a new GT estate was not enough to prevent its closure in May 1976.

After the gimmickiness of the Probe and the Siva, the *Daily Telegraph*/IBCAM stand revealed a respectable new piece of British styling, the 2+2 Cirrus coupé.

At Earls Court 1970 *Telegraph* magazine editor John Anstey had launched the British styling competition in conjunction with IBCAM, calling for a design of a 2+2 coupé which was to be built on the basis of a Ford Escort. The winning design would then actually be built for real, and the magazine managed to get the motor industry to fund it. Shown at the 1971 show, the winning design came from Michael Moore, a designer in what had been Rootes body engineering at Chrysler. Ford donated an Escort RS1600 and in five months before the 1972 show Woodall Nicholson, better known as hearse builders, created a smart coupé, the Cirrus, which earned Moore a job at Chrysler USA and he even got to keep the car. The brief for the next car, a family saloon on Austin Maxi mechanicals, had been issued at the 1971 show and the results would be seen next year.

1973

Oh dear, times were about to get hard. As the 1973 Earls Court Motor Show opened there was already talk of petrol rationing. Egypt and Syria had attempted to reclaim territory from Israel in surprise attacks on the holy day of Yom Kippur. Lasting only from 6 to 25 October, the war was short but its effects were long reaching. To punish the West for backing Israel, members of the Organisation of Arab Petroleum Exporting Countries (OPEC) launched an oil embargo and there were fuel shortages, a stock market crash and a global economic slowdown.

William Towns, by then a well-known British designer in his 1973 Minissima, which was looked at by Leyland for production. (Giles Chapman Picture Library)

The fuel crisis was to be most keenly felt in the US, but European countries had to introduce fuel and energy rationing. Worse still, industrial action brought a power cut to the 1973 press day which meant several stands were not able to produce the usual cooked breakfast for their guests, who had to just drink the champagne. Most of the cafeterias had to close.

Outside, Friends of the Earth were protesting against the car – 'Bring back the bus! All is forgiven!' whilst inside two young ladies

(in trouser suits, *Motor* noted) briefly waved a banner above a Rolls-Royce protesting about Britain's arms embargo on the Middle East having spare parts for tanks.

For enthusiasts the star of the 1973 show was the AC 3000ME sports car. After a decade of the mighty Cobra and vast-bonneted American-engined V8 monsters it unveiled a mid-engined two-seater prototype powered by a Ford 3-litre V6 attached to AC's own design of gearbox. The design had been seen the year before at the Racing Car Show as the Diablo, with a Maxi engine. By then AC had acquired the rights.

Orders flooded in for the 3000ME but what followed was a Motor Show saga, with a slightly changed version reappearing every year until 1979, when it finally went on sale. Only seventy-one were built to 1984. The fuel crisis hadn't helped but, above all, AC Managing Director Derek Hurlock blamed safety regulations introduced in 1976, just as the car was ready. 'There's no question that type approval killed our hopes for the car,' Hurlock told Mark Hughes in 1986 for *Classic and Sportscar*. 'We had to crash two or three cars, and invest a great deal in re-design. And every time we submitted a modification to the authorities that cost even more.' AC was largely kept afloat by its contract to supply the rather nasty blue three-wheeled 'invalid' cars for the disabled.

The kit-car industry was dealt a fatal blow in 1973 with the introduction of Value Added Tax (VAT) to most goods and services at 10 per cent. This meant that even a car in component form attracted tax on all its parts and the old saving on purchase tax was lost. Sports car fans bade farewell to getting a Lotus Elan on the cheap and building it over a weekend. Clan and Gilbern were out of business by the following year. TVR skipped the show.

British Leyland was back with a full cupboard of new cars. There was a wrongly timed V8 engine for the MGB GT, a sixteen-valve cylinder head engine for the Triumph Dolomite Sprint (when such engines were rare), a coupé version of the Jaguar XJ and the show centrepiece Austin Allegro.

Having allowed the Austin-Morris 1100/1300 range to languish without much development for over ten years (then again it was still selling nicely), BL had launched its successor in May 1973. There was a transverse front-driving engine as before and Austin being the 'technology' brand allowed the Allegro to have a new type of suspension system, called Hydragas: taking the idea of the 1960s

The 1973 Austin Maxi-based Aquila was the most intelligent IBCAM/ *Daily Telegraph* styling study and the last. (Giles Chapman Picture Library)

Hydrolastic system, where interconnected fluid-filled chambers replaced coil springs and were meant to level the ride front to rear. In Hydragas, nitrogen replaced rubber as the springing medium, although the fluid was still present. It was a good selling point; 'needs no maintenance', said the voice on the TV adverts as a startled showroom customer was whisked around a quarry. Versions of Hydragas were used in BL and Rover cars until 2002.

A great deal of ink has been spilt over the years to explain how rubbish the Allegro was (exaggerated by instances of the poor build which plagued BL cars), but it was well received at first. The styling, by Harris Mann, was rather more rounded than his initial styling sketches with barrel sides and inset headlamps, but it was individual and held far fewer of the rust traps the 1100 had fostered. One pointless gimmick was the 'Quartic' steering wheel, squared off at the corners, soon dropped after it was revealed that the Metropolitan Police had replaced the wheels on their Panda Allegros with round ones. Sporty Allegros and the 1974 Vanden Plas 1500 had round steering wheels and others followed.

This was a car for Europe, said Lord Stokes. Britain had joined the Common Market on 1 January 1973. Membership applications in 1963 and 1967 had failed, it was reported, due to French President Charles de Gaulle's objections to English becoming the common language of Europe. But unlike its European competitors, the one big thing the Allegro lacked was a hatchback, even though the shape suggested it. This feature was apparently only reserved for the Maxi in the BL plan. However, the engine choice was broad, from 998cc A Series to the 1748cc Maxi unit.

Also on the 1973 Leyland stand was a not unattractive box on wheels called the Minissima. It was the work of William Towns, who had been freelancing from Aston Martin. The Minissima had a Mini engine and Mini 10in wheels but was shorter at 7ft 6in long and had a single rear door. It was just about a four-seater with two small inward-facing jump seats at the rear, pre-dating the Smart car genre by decades.

It had started life in 1972 as the Townscar, pitched as a Mini replacement. British Leyland brought the prototype and re-badged it Minissima as an attraction for its 1973 show stand but did nothing more with it. To be fair, it would have required a great deal of development and having only one exit to the rear was not a good safety feature. The Minissima did eventually reach production enlarged with extra doors as the Elswick Envoy car for wheelchair users.

For an alternative take on Leyland's Maxi, Earls Court visitors could visit the IBCAM/*Daily Telegraph* Magazine stand to see the Aquila, winner of the 1971/72 British Styling Competition.

Designers had been asked for a blueprint for a family saloon of a style suitable for 1976 onwards based on the Austin Maxi mechanicals. British Leyland had agreed to supply the donor car, pay a large part of the winning design's build costs, transport it and arrange for publicity. One wonders how happy they were when it only drew attention to the rather plain looks of the regular Maxi. A plethora of British firms supplied other components.

Aquila was the work of Christopher Field from Devon, with thoroughly modern features such as plastic bumpers front and rear, headlamps behind transparent covers, electric windows and a windscreen with a built-in radio aerial. Its construction cost was rumoured to be £26,000. And that was the end of the *Telegraph*'s Motor Show cars. IBCAM had become disenchanted by the minimal financial contribution of the magazine, while Chrysler, the next donor supplier was not prepared to be as generous as British Leyland.

The 1974 show promised colourful family fun. Big cars from America and Australia are still hanging on (AMC then Chrysler, left) despite the fuel crisis. (SMMT/Olympia/LMA)

WISING UP TO SAFETY

I'It took a long time and ultimately legislation to make British car makers (and, to be fair, the public also) pay much attention to car safety. Volvo had invented the three-point seat belt in 1958 and, although in the same year some specialist coachbuilders had fitted belts to several Rolls-Royces and Bentleys at Earls Court, they didn't re-appear. Many considered belts constricting and untidy.

Nonetheless, in 1964 there were about thirthy-five brands of belts on the British market. In 1965 Britain required the fitting of seat belt anchorage points in new cars and by 1967 belts had to be fitted to front seats of new cars.

But even if you had been wearing a belt your car would most likely disintegrate or trap you. Enter American lawyer Ralph Nader, who caused a seismic shift in consumer awareness with his 1965 book *Unsafe at Any Speed*. Partially focussed on the handling deficiencies of the rear-wheel-drive Chevrolet Corvair, the book accused car manufacturers of cynical resistance to the introduction of safety features.

US legislators rushed to improve safety and emissions standards on domestic and imported cars, so European manufacturers who sold there had to invest or else withdraw. The early 1970s brought the influential American Experimental Safety Vehicle programme (ESV), where carmakers were invited to construct cars which could be crashed forwards or backwards at 50mph, sideways at 25mph and rolled at over 70mph without hurting the (non-belted) occupants. The first ESV cars were to be produced in 1972 and exhibited in Washington.

They were all requirements likely to become future law. American manufacturers reluctantly set to building prototypes which weighed anything up to 3 tons and European manufacturers who wanted to sell in America, chiefly Volkswagen (the Beetle was a prime target for Nader), invested heavily in their own ESVs, while noting that it would be a better idea to actually compel people to wear seatbelts. British Leyland fielded the MG SSV-1, based on an MGB GT, with the help of British component makers. Features included twin airbags, low rubber-faced bumpers and braking lights which flashed according to the severity of braking. All of these were actually adopted decades later, unlike the huge wide-angle periscope mirror perched on the roof. Further Leyland safety cars in 1974 were based on the Mini, the Morris Marina and Austin 1800.

From 1973 US regulations demanded that all vehicles should have bumpers capable of withstanding a 5mph impact without damaging the bodywork or lamps and a 2½mph impact at the rear (raised to 5mph for 1975). Saab was already in production with such a moulded bumper mounted on its 99 which could recover its shape after bumps up to 3mph. Other Swedish makes followed suit, plus notably MG, heavily dependent on US sales, controversially restyled the front and rear of its cars to incorporate 'rubber' bumpers of Bayflex 90 polyurethane over steel and foam on reinforced body mounting points.

At this time, British counter-argument to the American style of safety legislation – in fact to British safety legislation – was that if you made cars which handled and braked well drivers would get into fewer accidents anyway. It was often said that more people died from smoking than road accidents and that in the USA the murder rate was near the fatal accident rate. By 1970 only one in three British front-seat occupants would actually wear a seatbelt if there was one. It took ten years of parliamentary argument from 1973 until the wearing of front seatbelts became compulsory in the UK.

The 1974 Morris Marina-based SRV2 was one of four cars built by Leyland to showcase safety features. (LAT)

Ferraris are shined at the 1974 show: the 308GTB, right, had just
replaced the Dino. (www.paykanhunter.com)

The Lotus Esprit was the firm's 1975 showstopper, about to become a Bond car. (Lotus)

The SMMT celebrated the sixtieth show with landmark cars, but 1975 was its penultimate Earls Court year. (SMMT, courtesy of Coventry History Centre)

BP BUILD-A-CAR

Something even odder than the 1974 flying Bond car (p.113) could be found on the stand next to it: the top three winners of the British Petroleum (BP) Build-a-Car competition. Replacing the BP hovercraft building competition, technically minded students had been asked to design a city car with the results judged on environmental, ergonomic, construction and performance criteria. The big prize was a Leyland minibus. The competition was jointly organised with the Corps of Royal Electrical and Mechanical Engineers which put the tiny cars through a weekend of testing and breaking down before invited judges – including William Towns of Aston Martin – chose the winner.

The 1974 winner was Cranleigh School from Surrey with a boxy Citroën 2CV-engined car. They returned two years later with an improved version, when the requirements had got even tougher. Only twenty-two of the forty-five schools which started the competition made the finals.

The class of 1976 included The Wasp, from Broadlands School in Norfolk, which was entirely circular with two scooter engines, two steering wheels and two seats. It had to end the test day being pushed but won £75 for ingenuity. The winner, Citica, was more conventional but sat four in comfort and worked. It was created by four boys from Radyr Comprehensive in Cardiff without funds but with twenty-five sponsors and parts they had scrounged from scrap cars, chiefly a 300cc Isetta bubble car engine. The BP Build-a-Car competition became something of an institution, lasting into the 1990s with BP still involved in school car designing in 2015.

The boys from Radyr Comprehensive celebrate victory in the 1976 BP Build-a-Car competition. Part of the prize was a slot at Earls Court. (BP)

Opposite: The Aston Martin Lagonda took a long time to mature from its 1976 surprise unveiling; first deliveries were not until 1979. (Aston Martin)

Above: The 1976 Rover 3500, also known as the SD1, arrived to great acclaim for its distinctive styling. (Author's collection)

Right: Noted British cartoonist and illustrator Martin Honeysett often saw the funny side of the Earls Court Motor Show. (Penny Precious)

Earls Court reinvents the car show as Motorfair in 1977. The red Chrysler Sunbeam in front seems to be making a bid for freedom. (Olympia/LMA)

Inside, and all is Monaco: real palm trees and a motley collection of vehicles. The space capsule-like object in the centre is Doctor Who's Whomobile. (Olympia/LMA)

The 1978 NEC Motor Show featured a perky cartoon car and truck called the 'Brums', slang for Birmingham. The biggest ever crowd engulfs the British Leyland exhibit. Ford had no cars for its stand due to industrial action. (Author's collection/LAT)

The vast column-free space of Earls Court 2, pictured in 2006. (Olympia)

Regularly refurbished, C. Howard Crane's 1937 design is looking smart in 2005. (Olympia)

September 2014: a new Jaguar XE is escorted by two 1960s Mk II Jaguar police cars into the Earls Court Arena to a show for 3,000 guests. (Jaguar)

The new era: Goodwood's outdoor motor show, the Festival of Speed, was chosen for the UK premieres of the C4 Cactus and C1 in 2014. (Citroën)

Motor Show nostalgia in full swing at the 2008 Goodwood recreation of dollybird days. (Goodwood)

Vauxhall had been making determined efforts to brush off its 'old man' image with Dealer Team Vauxhall racing and showed a racing Ventora with a V8 engine but the centrepiece of its stand was a silver Firenza coupé (a two-door Viva with sloping rear) made a great deal more dynamic by the addition of a swooping nosecone made by Specialised Mouldings, a 131bhp 2.3-litre engine tuned by its racing partner Blydenstein and five-speed ZF gearbox. Into production the following year as the High Performance (HP) Firenza coupé, it was straight away nicknamed the 'Droopsnoot' but only around 200 would be made. The flat headlamps and sloping front had, however, given Vauxhall stylists inspiration on how to modify the upcoming new Opel models it was to sell.

Lamborghini once again overshadowed Ferrari – showing the new Bertone-styled Dino 2+2 and the beautiful 365GT Berlinetta Boxer – with the look-at-me Countach, now on sale in the UK for a mere £16,314, which was more than the costliest Rolls. First seen in 1971 and featuring a mid-mounted V12 said to be capable of propelling it to 170mph and doors which scissorred upwards, the Countach would be a 1970s and '80s schoolboy poster favourite.

Destined to be forgotten, General Motors had shipped in two very stylish experimental cars based on the Corvette, the two and four rotor, with Wankel rotary engines. The concept still held some fascination in those last pre-fuel-crisis days. Some styling features appeared on later Corvettes but the concepts were destined to be museum pieces.

By December 1973 the British government had ordered shops, offices and public spaces to cut lighting by half. A blanket 50mph speed limit was imposed the same month. Its economic policy also provoked a miners' strike and on 1 January 1974 a three-day working week was instigated to save coal at power stations. The price of petrol rocketed. In 1973 it was 38p a gallon and 73p by 1975. Buyers immediately wanted economical cars (sales of the venerable Mini shot up) and the glamorous but fuel-guzzling GTs of the early 1970s looked a completely different proposition. The much-lauded Jaguar XJ12 did around 14mpg. The speed limit was lifted in May 1974 but re-imposed in December with 50mph for single carriageways, 60 for dual, which stayed in force until May 1977. The motor industry complained that the motorist was being discriminated against when of the 1972 annual UK oil consumption of 102 million barrels petrol had accounted for 15.6.

Earls Court Ltd's management structure had been through major change in 1972. Property developer Jeffrey Sterling, through Sterling Guarantee Trust, bought the Earls Court Exhibition Centre, both land and property assets, for £4.4 million. In 1973 he snapped up Olympia for £11.4 million. The plan was to redevelop both sites for smaller-scale exhibitions while a new Earls Court was built, and Olympia would then close. It was accepted as inevitable that the Motor Show would move to the National Exhibition Centre.

However, the scheme was stalled by the oil crisis. Britain was beset by power cuts and strikes, property values dropped and Sterling's plans were shelved. He opted instead to concentrate on rebuilding the business of both his London halls, merging them into Earls Court and Olympia Ltd (ECO).

1974

The world's motor industry was in a tailspin by autumn 1974. Manufacturers who a year before had been planning large-engined luxury cars with plenty of weight to meet crash test requirements now had to divert their attention to economical cars. Despite praise for its product, Aston Martin had made a bumpy transition into the 1970s, the David Brown organisation having to sell it to new owners in 1972. Then came the oil crisis. In a bid to extend its range, 1974 saw the revival of the Lagonda name on a four-door version of the V8, but only seven were made.

Volkswagen's timing could not have been better, launching its all-new hatchback Golf, the real Beetle replacement, into the midst of the energy crisis. Benefitting from a later start than rivals such as the Fiat 128, Renault 5, Peugeot 104, Honda Civic, Datsun Cherry and Austin Allegro, the Golf's Italian styling concealed thorough engineering innovation such as a deceptively simple but effective rear suspension. It broke the air-cooled rear-drive mould and rescued the company. By autumn 1974 it was the best-selling car in West Germany. Although shown at Earls Court, British buyers did not get hold of right-hand drive Golfs until early 1975, restricted to 1.1-litre versions until the second half of the year, when the 1.5-litre arrived. With the pound weak against the Deutschmark, a UK Golf 1100 L didn't present itself as good value at £1,538, but over 17,000 were sold to British buyers in 1975.

The early 1970s saw a concerted London bombing campaign by the Irish Republican Army (IRA). After a telephone warning allowed the area to be cleared a device went off at the January 1974 Boat Show. (Mirrorpix)

Citroën too was on a roll. The GS was selling like hotcakes and while it was not a good time to launch big saloons the new CX replaced the DS after almost twenty years' production. It took much of the SM's advanced hydropneumatic suspension and braking system and although missing the rotary engine it was designed to take still impressed by having its DS-derived four-cylinder mounted transversely. At the other end of the price list, Citroën Cars Ltd of Slough's smartest move was to re-introduce the 2CV back into the UK, absent since 1959. This was the right car at the right time, charming and cheap. Advertising depicted it as a happy cartoon: at

£829.53 the 'world's cheapest car with a sunroof' and 46mpg-plus fuel economy.

Its kit car days behind it, Lotus bet the bank on the new Elite of 1974. This was the complete break with the kit-car past, the curtain raiser to a range of larger and more sophisticated cars for the 1970s and '80s. It was a car of many (perhaps too many) firsts for Lotus: first to offer four genuine seats for adults, first to use the new VARI vacuum resin moulding process, first to use the all-Lotus 2-litre sixteen-valve engine (already equipped to meet US emissions regulations) and first to be aimed straight at Britain's executive car market. The Elite was to have a full quota of luxury items such as electric windows and the option of air conditioning.

Apart from Mazda, most manufacturers were putting the brakes on rotary engines, but a trio of German cars were ahead of a trend which didn't take hold fully until the next decade: the turbocharged engine. In simple terms a turbocharger (hitherto in very limited car use) is a forced induction device pushing waste gases in the exhaust system into the engine for more efficient combustion and more power under load. It remains a way of extracting more power on demand without having to change to a larger engine capacity, or a way to reduce the engine size for economy, as happened in the 2000s. Early turbochargers suffered from 'lag', a gap under acceleration where nothing happened until they boosted in a surge and threw inexperienced drivers into hedges.

BMW, becoming a very desirable brand for British buyers, introduced the 2002 Turbo, boasting an exciting 170bhp in a small saloon festooned with motor sport bodykit. Not the car for a speed-restricted Europe it was only available in left-hand drive at £4,221 – more than a Jaguar E-Type. British tuner Broadspeed, which had been turbocharging Ford Capris, was entrusted by Opel to create the Manta Turbo, with a claimed 0–60mph time of 6.7 seconds and a sticker price of £3,492. The ultimate turbo of 1974 though was the 3.0-litre 256bhp Porsche 911 Turbo.

If turbos made a car fly, filmmakers also did. Tucked away at the rear of the main hall there was the 'James Bond flying car' brought to you courtesy of London Broadcasting, on air at the show studio nearby. The second Roger Moore Bond film, *The Man with the Golden Gun* was set to premiere on 19 December and here was the American Motors Corporation Matador used by villain Christopher Lee with jet engine and a massive wing. The show catalogue stated

Passing traffic warden Jacqui Smith peers at the AMC Matador 'flying car' from the 1974 James Bond film *The Man with the Golden Gun*. (Mirrorpix)

that 'already fourteen inquiries have been received from Middle East Sheikhs for similar cars.' Had they waited for the film to come out they would have seen the only car which did fly was a small radio-controlled one.

1975

A bumper year for genuinely new cars, 1975 was 'the penultimate annual Earls Court show' and it celebrated its Diamond Jubilee (of the 1905 Olympia show) with a display of motoring landmarks. The finance for staging the show was increased by £75,000 to a total of £350,000 and the landscape from the balconies looked a little different too, with stand height restrictions relaxed; Renault,

for example, had a two-storey display. This was nothing compared to Leyland, taking up almost half of the central block but mixing all its brands together, showing its vast range. The centrepiece was a turntable onto which five models were transported on and off by rails for individual shows of their features. *Motor* straightaway likened it to a British Rail shunting yard.

But British Leyland was in spectacular trouble. Its strategy for moving upmarket had failed; its sprawling empire of factories were militant and barely manageable. In 1974 it made a total loss of £23.9 million, and in 1975 the Labour government was forced to guarantee its working capital, effectively nationalising it. The government commissioned Sir Don Ryder to report on the company's current and future prospects, which he did in April 1975. He concluded that BL was simply too big to fail and recommended an incredible

The 1975 British Leyland 'shunting yard' turntable showing the new entrants. Anticlockwise from centre spot: Austin Allegro estate, Jaguar XJS, Princess and Triumph TR7. Beyond the stand, the new Vauxhall Cavalier. (LAT)

£1,500 million of public money be invested in modernisation, and that the company rationalise it products.

At the top of the current Leyland tree the Jaguar XJ-S had replaced the E-Type, to much discussion. As Jaguar believed at the time, as many carmakers did, that US regulations would outlaw the convertible, the XJ-S first appeared only as a fixed-head coupé with rear-end styling, which was not to all tastes. Its vast bonnet hid the magnificent Jaguar V12 engine and the cabin provided surprisingly snug accommodation for four to cross continents in speed and silence. It was not the sports car Jaguar enthusiasts had been hoping for to replace the E-Type, and sales only became respectable the following decade when smaller, more fuel-efficient engines became available.

The new Triumph TR7 also provoked sports car debate, marking the end of the TR convertibles which had begun in the 1950s. This fixed-head coupé offered two comfortable seats, a large boot and

a 2.0-litre Triumph Dolomite engine (sadly not the 16-valve) but its styling had the traditionalists most up in arms. Leyland designer Harris Mann had produced a pronounced wedge-shaped car with impact-absorbing bumpers and pop-up headlamps. Traditional Triumph it was not, but it was right in line with Italian sports car styling trends. The TR7 was aimed straight at the US market and at first sold so well that British production was held until 1976. TV adverts showed it breaking out of a wedge-shaped box. Success soured, though, in the wake of quality problems at the Liverpool factory.

Nobody had applied wedge styling to a large family saloon, but Leyland must have seemed to be wedge-mad in 1975, as a new car replaced the Austin 1800 Series, looking like nothing else on the road. Again styled in-house by Harris Mann with reference to his 1969 Zanda design, by the time of the Earls Court show its name had changed since its spring launch. Although Lord Stokes had said badge engineering was over, the new large car went on sale in March 1975 as the 18:22 Series of the Morris 1800, Austin 2200 and Wolesley 18/22, even though there was very little interest in this elderly brand by now, complete with velour trimmings and a little radiator grille with the trademark illuminated badge.

The 18/22 had a six-cylinder 2.2-litre engine driving the front wheels and the 1800 offered four-cylinders. Although the shape was crying out for it, a hatchback was again absent as on the Allegro. BL marketeers claimed that it would have harmed sales in the 'executive' market into which it was aimed, but it is more likely that they believed it would conflict with the five-door Rover SD1, due out in 1976. Proving it could be done, Torcars of Plymouth offered to convert existing Princesses to hatchbacks and in 1980 Leyland gave in and the restyled and renamed Ambassador gained a fifth door.

It was received as a good-looking spacious car with a good ride, courtesy of Hydragas. However, customers faced long waits for their cars as Leyland's Cowley plant was beset by strikes in the spring and summer, and in September the whole range was renamed Princess in an attempt at the rationalisation the Ryder Report had recommended. The only way to distinguish a Princess 1800 from a 2200 was by a change from four headlamps to a pair of square units. The honeymoon was sadly short as early quality problems were amplified by a press and public keen for a bit of 'Leyland bashing'. Failing driveshafts earned it TV coverage.

One way to mitigate shoddily built cars was to offer a blinding warranty package and in 1975 BL launched Supercover. By the standards of the 2010s it seems minimal, but back then new Leyland owners with Supercover cars were treated to an unlimited-mileage twelve-month warranty instead of 12,000 miles and free AA membership. Ford and Chrysler soon improved theirs.

Of Leyland's domestic competitors, Ford had introduced its second-generation Escort during 1975 looking no different from its German-made version – apart from the prototype RS2000 with its own 'droopsnoot' – but Vauxhall at Luton had been allowed some leeway to create a distinct identity for its version of the Opel Kadett, the Vauxhall Chevette, launched in May. At first a neat three-door hatchback, the Chevette was technically unadventurous with a 1.3-litre Viva engine and rear-wheel drive, but in place of the Kadett's flat front was a sloping 'droopsnoot' with no visible radiator

The Russian Moskvitch estate might have been crude but it was a big tough barge for the price of a Mini. (Giles Chapman Picture Library)

grille and flat rectangular headlamps. Its sales success took Vauxhall by surprise and production was increased and plusher trim levels added. At this time both Opel and Vauxhall cars were sold in the UK, the Opels marginally more expensive.

The big Vauxhall surprise of the show was the launch of the Vauxhall Cavalier, ready for November sale. Essentially it was the Opel Ascona with a new Vauxhall nose, a rear-wheel-drive saloon slightly smaller than the Cortina but meant to bridge the gap between the Viva and the large and unsuccessful Victor. Available with 1.6- and 1.9-litre engines, the Cavalier range lacked an estate but offered smart two and three-door coupés.

All well and good, but the problem was this new car with a British badge was made in (gasp) Belgium at a time when British manufacturers were hysterical about imports and 'buying British' – some companies would only buy British-built fleet cars. Vauxhall at Luton had wanted its version of the General Motors U Car in a hurry and was reportedly in two minds whether to show a Belgian Cavalier at Earls Court at all in the face of union unhappiness and newspaper outrage. At the show it admitted the final decision to

Panther was the top of British bling in the 1970s. The 1975 de Ville hid the fact that its doors came from a Leyland 1800/Maxi. (Giles Chapman Picture Library)

launch the Cavalier in October had only been made in August 1975 but denied there were any plans to drop car production in the UK. All this aside, it immediately found sales success and Luton Cavalier saloon production started in 1977.

As if the Japanese invasion wasn't bad enough, those Eastern European, or rather communist, cars were attracting more and more private buyers who wanted more car for their hard-earned cash, even if it was a bit outdated. In 1974 the Lada had arrived, a Russian version of the recently defunct Fiat 124. In October 1974 a Lada 1200 cost a headline-grabbing £999. In 1975 came the Polski Fiat, from Poland of course, based on the Fiat 125 but minus its twin-cam engine.

Other countries liked Lada too: in 1974 West Germany took 2,400 and 10,000 in 1975. In Britain, Polski Fiat, Lada and Skoda grew their sales by 53 per cent during the first nine months of 1975, way ahead of the Japanese. Moskvitch and Wartburg were still there bringing up the rubbish corner, although the latter model was obsolete, banned by European emissions laws. A Polski Fiat 125P saloon cost £1,349 all in, for which you got a smart-looking (courtesy of 1960s Fiat styling)

family car with four doors and a big boot. A two-door Escort Popular was the same amount but stripped down to the last grommet to save money.

'Their prices are totally unrealistic in relation to the true cost of manufacture,' railed the SMMT, but the Lada Car Company's managing director pointed out Russians had to pay a very high rate of purchase tax, just like Britons in the 1950s. Nonetheless, the Polski Fiat creaked on until 1991 in the UK and the Lada 1200's successor, the Riva, until 1997.

Chrysler – formerly Rootes – hadn't been able to field an all-new car since the 1970 Hillman Avenger but for 1975 there was the Chrysler Alpine, a roomy five-door hatchback which had been styled in Coventry but owed its engine to Simca in France, where the car was badged as a Simca. As right-hand-drive Alpines started production on the opening day of the show, French orders for the Simca were apparently coming in at 1,000 a day. British Alpines were built in Coventry from 1976.

Lotus once again pulled off a showstopper in the shape of the beautiful Lotus Esprit two-seater, which had made its debut at Paris the previous month. Its shape wasn't entirely a surprise but a production translation of an Italdesign show car seen at the 1972 Turin show. Its 2.0-litre Lotus 907 engine was in the same 160bhp tune as the Elite but in this lighter car good for a 124mph top speed when tested (a bit short of the claimed 138mph).

Like many small carmakers hit by the energy crisis, Lotus had been struggling to stay in business during 1975, at the expense of mass redundancies. Although the Esprit was shown in the autumn, the company did not have the tooling ready to put it into production. It was just as well that the Eclat, a booted version of the Elite and shown at the same time, was ready for sale. Customer Esprits were finally ready for delivery in June 1976, by which time the price had risen from a claimed £5,844 in Paris (in line with the cost of an Eclat) to £7,883. Thanks to the sheer doggedness of Lotus PR Don McLaughlan, a white Series 1 Esprit was immortalised as a submersible car in the 1977 James Bond film *The Spy Who Loved Me*.

Rolls-Royce was showing a 'mistletoe green' example of its second new model since the 1965 Silver Shadow, the vast and vastly expensive Camargue coupé. The two-door four-seat body was coach-built on a Silver Shadow platform by Mulliner Park Ward with styling by Pininfarina, which was not to all tastes. Its advanced features included automatic split-level air conditioning. A £31,500 price tag was no deterrent and even before its introduction into the US in April 1976 a 'nearly new' Camargue was going for £35,000.

Panther also seemed to be sailing expensively on past the fuel crisis and by show time had made eleven four-door saloon de Villes at £21–22,000 each. Its two-tone paintwork mimicked Bugatti style from the 1930s and the luxurious interior was complete with cocktail cabinet. Panthers had become a favourite in oil-rich countries and tapped a wave of British fashion for all things 1930s (many a de Ville was a wedding car).

Although TVR's obligatory topless model was told to do her business quickly on press day, the 1975 Earls Court Motor Show marked the company's triumphant return from a factory fire with an unexpected prototype 3000M Turbo, developed over the year with a conversion by Broadspeed.

1976

It was the end of an era. The 61st London International Motor Show organised by the SMMT was the last in an unbroken series that had run every year since 1948. There would be no SMMT show in 1977 and the National Exhibition Centre beckoned. However, to the rescue came the *Daily Express*. 'The glitter of the 1976 London Motor Show has been slightly dimmed by the decision of the Society of Motor Manufacturers and Traders not to hold it again in 1977 and then to move it to the National Exhibition Centre in Birmingham in 1978,' wrote its motoring editor David Benson in the guide to 1977 cars. 'But fortunately the directors of the *Daily Express* have taken the courageous decision that the London show must go on.'

No tears shed in this *Motor* magazine editorial: 'Farewell Earls Court, roll on the Birmingham National Exhibition Centre. Motorfair or not next year (courtesy of the entrepreneurial *Daily Express* and MAA) we will not be the only ones sorry to end a long association with the gloomy grottos of Earls Court.'

There were over 300 cars including sixty models from a dozen countries. A ticket was yours for 80p every day apart from opening day, when it was £2.50. As usual, motor caravans were tucked away in Pembroke Hall, and upstairs, aside from furry dice which

dangled from the rear view mirrors and seat covers, there were some accessories that would have made motoring a lot more pleasant and which are seen as essentials in today's cars. The new-car buyer of 1976 expected their car to come off the production line with a heated rear window, reversing lamps and exterior mirrors, but a record hot summer had people dreaming of air conditioning by Alpinair, cruise control for any make of car from around £60 from Econocruise, or just an electric door mirror from Autosafe.

But this final international show boasted a significant debut, the second four-door Aston Martin Lagonda since 1974 but with futuristic square-edged styling by William Towns with pop-up headlamps. it was unveiled to the press on 12 October – only eighteen months after the company had been bought from the receiver by yet another group of owners, who produced the prototype new Lagonda in ten months. The show car was a non-runner.

The 5.3-litre V8 engine was familiar but the car's reliance on electronic operation for many systems drew as much wonderment as the styling. A digital dashboard converted everything from speed (switchable between miles and kilometres) to fuel consumption and tiny pressure switches operated items such as the windscreen wipers, gear selection and window opening.

The projected price was £20,000 and come show end the Sheikh of Qatar was said to have ordered three and the company was confident of selling 100 a year. Getting the electronics to behave themselves slowed development. In its September 1978 edition *Car* magazine noted that the first car to be delivered in April to the Marchioness of Tavistock was withdrawn when it couldn't be driven. Production started in late 1978 at one a week.

Restyled in 1987 with rounded-off edges and a re-designed nose where six smaller lights replace the pop-up headlamps, 645 Lagonda chassis were built before the end of production in 1989.

The British Leyland 'shunting yard' returned, taking up 27,000 sq. ft of floor space, with a viewing theatre and three turntables onto which eight different cars shunted themselves, controlled by an operator. The centrepiece was the new five-door Rover 3500 or, as it has become known, the SD1, standing for Leyland's Specialist Car Division, which swept away the old Rover P6 and the Triumph 2000/2500 models in one go. Styled in-house by David Bache, the nose bore a strong resemblance to the Ferrari Daytona and its interior discarded the traditional Rover wood for beige padded plastics and velour upholstery which apparently passed the 'minking' test of not pulling out hairs from expensive coats. Standard equipment included the novelty of central locking. Although the rear suspension was simplified compared to the P6, it had a self-levelling function. The car so impressed the critics that, like its predecessor, it won the Car of the Year title. Big cars were no longer bad news and a waiting list soon built up, exacerbated by getting the new factory in Solihull on line. Sadly like other Leyland cars, build quality took longer to catch up.

The new Ford Fiesta, Ford's first 'supermini', was conspicuously absent from Earls Court. European Fords had by now converged from differing designs for Germany or England into the same car during the 1970s but the launches were still wide apart. The new Cortina had been seen as the Ford Taunus the previous January and the Fiesta had been launched at Paris but was denied a London showing so as not to overexcite buyers as right-hand drive sales were not due until 1977. Cortina production was at a standstill due to strikes.

Domestic manufacturers like Leyland continued to give dire warnings over unfair competition from imports but that was clearly what people wanted to buy. Managing director Derek Whittaker said it could have sold more cars in the home market for 1976 had their not been so many production stoppages (i.e. strikes).

Datsun had its new Cherry at the show, sure to be a big seller, but such was the furore over imported cars that it wasn't given a noisy press launch. Equally discreet but more significant, Honda showed its new three-door Accord at £2,800. Honda had always been a cut above other Japanese brands for the quality of its engineering and so this first Accord was admired for its details, fit and finish plus European good looks compared to a Volkswagen Scirocco. A saloon would follow and it would become a best-selling world car, especially in America.

Curious cars included William Town's Microdot, at the other extreme to his Lagonda, taking the theme of the 1973 Minissima even smaller with a golf buggy-like car with three-abreast seating and no boot but a shopping trolley which slotted in the back bumper.

The electric car was represented by the Electraction EVR-1, the front end of a Vauxhall Chevette grafted awkwardly onto a small two-door passenger compartment. A 100-mile range was implausibly claimed, something which real electric cars were only achieving in 2015, and it was priced at £4,500, as much as a new Rover 3500. The brainchild of former Ford man Roy Haynes, the EVR-1 was pitched as prototype for development into an 'invalid carriage'.

Panther revealed that it had been supplanted as transport for Patrick McNee and Joanna Lumley in *The New Avengers* by Leyland rushing in and plying the producers with free Jaguars, Rovers, Triumphs and MGs. The consolation was the warm reception given to its new two-seat sports car, the Vauxhall-engined Lima. At the next, very different Earls Court Motor Show, Panther was set to be the true star.

6 THE SHOW MOVES ON
1977–2014

In October 1977, having lost its status as a venue for the British International Motor Show and with no chance of competing with the shiny new NEC, Earls Court became the *Daily Express* Motorfair, a giant motoring theme park. The roof of the Warwick Road entrance was festooned with a large merry-go-round on which a line of new cars appeared ready to go in circles.

Inside the orderly rows of stands had been abandoned to the theme of the show, Monte Carlo – on the basis of its motor sport connections. In the centre of the ground floor, part of the swimming pool was dropped by 9ft into Boat Show mode, onto which a replica of central Monaco's Hotel de Paris and Casino was erected at a cost of £250,000; its paint colour exactly matched the real thing. A 460ft, 6-ton road wound its way upwards to the roof, allowing display cars to travel onto the main 'square' where a 200-year-old palm tree joined others imported from the South of France.

This was the setting for thrice-daily Woolworths fashion shows from Pan's People (of *Top of the Pops* fame) and a Unipart Pit-Stop contest where teams of four contestants dressed in silly costumes tried to manoeuvre four giant spark plugs into Austin Allegros with 6ft spanners. Record-breaking and historic cars were sprinkled around the hall, there was a crèche and a play area for children, a clown car show, a giant Monaco Scalextric slot-car racing track and an 'Action Man' war games area. Gone were the scantily clad models, even on press day – this was a family show. You could take a class in car maintenance and try racing and crash test simulators. And see some new cars.

Not technically a motor show and held in association with the Motor Agents Association, Motorfair was billed as 'a selling show for all the family' because the stand space was occupied by consortiums of south-east new-car dealers, arranged by brand and supported by the manufacturers (albeit somewhat squeezed by Monaco square). However, all of the major names were present. Many of the new-car stands were operated by more than one dealer (Mazda's was a group of fifteen) but they worked out a system where the nearest local dealer got the sale.

The Leyland shunting yard was taking a break but the company's support and its dealers' money was essential for Motorfair, the fifty-five-car range taking the full length of one side of the hall. It was reported that had the London show not happened Leyland would have staged its own 1977 version at the NEC. It had opened its seven halls in 1976 and big shows poached included the Motor Show and Furniture Show. Olympia contracted in size and the Ideal Home moved to Earls Court for more space in 1978.

The first floor of Motorfair was devoted to accessories and used cars, with 100 a day anticipated to be sold and taken away each evening. Public car auctions took place in the Pembroke Hall, a novelty normally only reserved for trade buyers.

The pre-show hype verged on the hysterical. 'The show that should have happened years ago,' thundered *Motor* after an exciting press day (also open to public preview at £5 a ticket). and it decided that 'The future presentation of Motor Shows both in Britain and

The wraps are off the astonishing Panther 6 the night before Motorfair 1977. (LAT)

Earls Court's other life: June 1977 and members of the rock band *Queen* at rehearsals, from left to right: Roger Taylor, Freddie Mercury, Brian May and John Deacon. (Mirrorpix)

abroad is likely to be affected by the success or failure of the Earls Court Motorfair and it looks like being a major success.'

The surprise car of Motorfair was as extravagant as the fake Monaco. Only six weeks beforehand Panther had taken the wraps off Robert Jankel's most astonishing creation, the £39,950 Panther 6. A 16ft-long two-seater convertible with a vast rear deck which opened electrically to reveal an 8.2-litre V8 engine from the Cadillac Eldorado driving through an automatic gearbox, and behind it extra space for two spare wheels. Yes, two. The '6' came from two pairs of front wheels, following the 1976 Tyrrell P34 Formula 1 racecar. There was a claim that they made the car safer, clearing a dry stretch of road for the rear axle, but it was more for effect than improved handling. Pirelli custom-made the front tyres, which were smaller than the rears. To combat the engine's US emissions standard 190bhp, the 6 had twin turbochargers taking its power up to a claimed 600bhp. Fuel consumption was about 6mpg on a good day.

The aluminium bodywork was styled partly by Panther and by Vauxhall's head of styling Wayne Cherry, as one of Panther's contracts was to build its prototype cars. Despite its vast size, there was only space for three passengers (one in an extension of the driver's seat) in the leather-trimmed cockpit where they were treated to electric seats of every adjustment, powerful air conditioning, the best Blaupunkt sound system, a telephone and a Sinclair miniature television aimed away from the driver, who was given a digital dashboard display. The front section of bodywork contained the air conditioner (from a truck), a huge radiator and pop-up headlamps. 'We don't build motor show gimmicks,' Bob Jankel told a TV reporter at the show. 'All our cars we've shown have gone into production.'

Eight Panther 6s were said to have been ordered at the show, a hefty cash deposit required for each, to buyers from Panther's natural market: the Middle East but also America, Germany, Switzerland and Japan. HRH Princess Margaret, who opened the show, was noted to have spent far longer on the Panther stand than others. It was to be a magnificent folly; looking to mass-produce the Lima, the company ran into difficulties and in 1980 the receiver was called in when only two Panther 6s had been built. Panther was then bought by a Korean company.

The other new car of the show was more prosaic but more important. A struggling Chrysler UK had been given a government grant to keep the Scottish Linwood plant going with the demise of the Hillman Imp and brought the new hatchback Chrysler Sunbeam into production from a combination of Hillman Avenger underpinnings in a record nineteen months. 'Put a Chrysler Sunbeam in your life,' trilled Petula Clark in the adverts, but while it was regarded as a smart car it couldn't save Chrysler UK, sold to Peugeot in 1978, and itself axed in 1981.

Did Motorfair change the concept of motor shows forever? Not really. When it was time for the palm trees to be packed up, the statistics were described as 'respectable'. Over twelve days there were 401,349 visitors compared to almost 500,000 in 1976. Then again, they bought cars. Leyland sold 294 cars worth £1.5 million and Mazda almost 100. Ferrari sold twenty-five cars and TVR seven.

1978 AND BEYOND

Earls Court could never have competed with the sheer scale of the first Birmingham International Motor Show from 20–29 October 1978. A dedicated visitor could have stayed overnight at the on-site hotel and taken two days to tour the five halls. For the first time cars, commercial vehicles and caravans were shown together, over 700 exhibitors occupying 1 million sq. ft. All of the halls were on ground level, with, unlike Earls Court, plenty of natural light from glass panels at the tops of the walls. A purpose-built railway station, Birmingham International, delivered punters straight into the central 'piazza' where there were shops and a bank, plus restaurants and bars for each hall. Shuttle buses shipped visitors in from thousands of car-parking spaces.

Lucas sponsored a dedicated press centre but the motoring press was not uniformly pleased because they were still based in London and were not enthralled with having to trudge round another show on the scale of Frankfurt. 'In press terms, the NEC never attracted the same number of overseas press,' says Harry Calton, now heading Ford of Britain's press office. 'With respect, they didn't want to go to Birmingham. Earls Court had an appeal because it was in London, and there were theatres and everything else. And it was very convenient, they could fly in, spend three days in London and take in the show and do other things as well.' The paying public, though, loved the Birmingham show. This biggest British motor show drew the largest crowd ever of 913,000.

Tommy Sopwith, chairman of Earls Court Motorfair, had pledged it would be back in 1979, but it was not to return until 1981 as a 'regional motor show', then bi-annually from 1983, when the Motor Agents Association was partnered by the SMMT. There were still fashion shows but the extravagance of Monaco was never repeated. It settled down as a smaller alternative to the NEC show.

Earls Court held firm. The arrival of the NEC had inevitably lead to a re-examination of the exhibiting needs of London but in 1975 a report issued by the Confederation of British Industry and the London Chamber of Commerce and Industry recommended that Earls Court was still fit for purpose and in the short term would be more economically modernised and enlarged rather than the proposed schemes which included Docklands. It was still pulling in around 2 million visitors a year.

The Greater London Council granted Earls Court a £5 million grant to spruce up its facilities in 1979, the owners added a further £1.5 million and work started in 1982, which included a new sound system, better restaurants, moveable concert seating and new twin escalators.

The 1980s saw an upturn for both Earls Court and Olympia, the latter refitting its Empire Hall and renaming it Olympia 2. Sterling Guarantee Trust, which had merged with Olympia in 1973 to form ECO, merged with shipping company P&O in 1985, and by the mid 1990s Earls Court and Olympia were holding 165 events a year. The Earls Court Exhibition Centre supported about 500 full-time jobs.

The Ideal Home Show, Boat Show, Royal Tournament and Crufts dog show stayed in London through the 1990s and music continued to be a major part of Earls Court's offering. It played host to some of the biggest names in pop music from the 1970s to its closure, holding audiences of up to 20,000 for concerts by stars such as David Bowie, Pink Floyd, Elton John, Oasis and Madonna. From 1996 it became home to the British Phonographic Industry (BRIT) awards, and hosted a full decade between 2000 and 2010. It also played host to large-scale opera productions of *Tosca* and *Aida*.

While the old Earls Court building couldn't at first begin to compare to the NEC's square footage, after demolishing the Warwick Hall and giving up on the car-parking space it was able to open the completely new Earls Court 2 in 1991 with 17,000 sq. m of floor space, claimed to be enough to hold four jumbo jets. The £100 million building offered a 40 per cent increase in exhibition space and once more partially spanning West–East rail lines on 1,113 support piles, which had to be moveable in case of future road and rail changes.

Earls Court 2 opened for Motorfair 1991 and once more London became a serious venue to see new cars. It was renamed the London Motor Show in 1993 and settled into a biannual run which ended abruptly in 2001 when, with only weeks to go before the show opened, it was cancelled by organiser Clarion. The closure was blamed on events in the wake of economic difficulties and defections which included Ford, MG Rover and Volkswagen.

And that was it for new cars at Earls Court, although from 2009 a car show of sorts returned, the biannual MPH Prestige & Performance Motor Show, later rebranded as the stunt-packed Top Gear Live and shared with the NEC.

But as the first decade of the new millennium drew on, the traditional British motor show stalled. Manufacturers preferred Frankfurt or Paris for a big launch rather than Birmingham. 'The overall travel would be towards decline,' says motoring journalist Richard Bremner. 'I think there would have been a couple of spikes, for example 1998 when the Rover 75 and Jaguar S-Type were launched at the same time. That was quite an important show, which would have drawn in overseas journalists but I think that was the last time it ever had any real significance internationally.'

Tradition was broken when the 2004 NEC show was moved to May/June to avoid a clash with Paris and allow visitors to enjoy outdoor experiences, but its star was fading. In 2006 London regained the British International Motor Show after the new ExCeL venue in Docklands out-bid Birmingham. ExCeL had opened in 2000 and gained the Boat Show in 2004. SMMT chief executive said, 'We believe a move to ExCeL will build on the show's rich history, giving the Motor Show a platform that will reclaim its international reputation as a premier league event,' and granted International Motor Industry Events Ltd a ten-year licence to organise the biennial show.

All seemed well after the 2006 event posted a final visitor tally of an Earls Court-like 420,000, a claimed 23 per cent increase on visitor numbers for the last NEC show. The 2008 British International Motor Show, from 23 July to 3 August, boasted twenty-three global debuts (notably the Lotus Evora) and more than fifty models were claimed to be making their first European or UK appearance. Sixty manufacturers were exhibiting, including an 'electric vehicle village' and 'heritage' section. Again a respectable 472,300 people visited but, in a telling sign of the way things were going, Volkswagen decided not to exhibit, along with its other mass-market brand Skoda.

It was to be the last British Motor Show. In the wake of an economic downturn, in March 2009 the SMMT announced it was cancelling the 2010 show. SMMT chief executive Paul Everitt said:

The British International Motor Show has been a tremendously successful showcase for the UK motor industry. In recent years the show has played a less important role in influencing new car buyers and vehicle manufacturers are focussing their limited resources on events and activities that have a more direct impact on brand awareness and consumer decisions.

The only similar British survivor was the London Motorexpo, a free car show where manufacturers sprinkled high-end models around the buildings of Canary Wharf and offered test drives but by 2016 it too was gone. A new-style London Motor Show was promised for May 2016 in Battersea Park, but there was initial scepticism that it was going to be viable.

Globally, carmakers were wondering how much bang they got from their buck at traditional motor shows, a debate which continued beyond economic downturns. Henry Foy, writing in the *Financial Times* in May 2014, identified an industry highly sceptical of spending vast sums flying journalists to shows around the world then entertaining them in relation to what they could get by more selective marketing. There were eighteen major international shows in 2014 but the 2013 Bologna and Melbourne events had been cancelled through lack of interest. Hi-tech cars were also being launched at smaller non-car specific events such as technology shows. 'Ten years ago, if you needed to sell a car, you would have to show it all over the world,' a nameless marketing director told the *Financial Times*. 'Nowadays everybody can see it immediately. The internet has made the car show obsolete from a product point of view.'

After the decline of Leyland and the collapse of Rover, the British motor industry had revived by 2014, now largely in foreign ownership (Japanese, German, American and Indian), hosting seven mainstream car manufacturers and eight premium and sports car makers. It built 1.5 million cars – the same number built in 1974.

And the British car buyer was an entirely different animal, unwilling to queue for hours and pay to be squashed into a hall full of cars which never moved. The internet was bursting with new car reviews and advice, old-style television road-test programmes had been replaced by free video reviews from anybody who could hold a camera and the carmakers could reach a global audience with a well-aimed launch on their own websites. 'There's all kinds of research to show that people have done most of their research about what they're going to buy even before they set foot in a dealership,' Richard Bremner observes. 'They've probably narrowed even to one car and they just want a confirmatory prod before they close the deal, or play one dealer off against another. Cars are more of a commodity than they once were. They're less excited about them although still concerned about buying the right one.'

The giant Frankfurt and Paris shows remained in the calendar – in 2013 Frankfurt drew over 800,000 visitors. But if you wanted to charge British enthusiasts money to see new cars, it seemed they had to be moving ones, and one venue came to represent the most successful post-British Motor Show offering: Goodwood.

Staged every summer since 1993, in the grounds of the 10th Duke of Richmond's Goodwood House in West Sussex, the Goodwood Festival of Speed, founded by his son Lord March, offered the chance to see new and historic race and performance cars power up a 1.16-mile hill climb. There were events and displays around the grounds and visitors could almost rub shoulders with past and present motor sport celebrities.

From 2009 the weekend was preceded by a one-day event on the Thursday, the Moving Motor Show, where members of the public (albeit pre-booked and probably likely sales prospects) could test drive new models on the hill-climb route. In 2015 twenty manufacturers exhibited, including Aston Martin, Ford, Ferrari and Peugeot. Tickets were £30 a head.

From 1998 the Festival of Speed was joined by the September Goodwood Revival weekend, repeated each year since. Pre-1966 competition cars once again raced on the revived circuit over a weekend. The recreation of the period went way beyond the cars on the track; to create a distinct atmosphere visitors dressed in pre-1966 clothes with great enthusiasm and those with the correct age of classic car could park on site for free. With each year the Revival's status and size grew, pulling in worldwide visitors, ever more expensive and rare racing cars and motoring celebrities. Car manufacturers with an interest in their own heritage saw it as a place to be.

With the dressing up came period entertainment and buildings around the track were dressed up to become shops and garages. In 2008 the Revival got its very own Earls Court Motor Show, a sign of some fond nostalgia. An aircraft hangar was given an art-deco frontage reminiscent of the Warwick Road original but inside the event was allowed to break out of its 'period' timeframe for manufacturers to display post-1966 vehicles. In the year of opening, exhibitors included Maserati, Jaguar, BMW, Ford and Rolls-Royce. There was a small historical connection: the 3rd Duke of Richmond had owned a house and farm on the Earls Court estate from 1802 to 1806.

According to the organisers, the 2014 three-day Goodwood Festival of Speed drew in 200,000 and the Moving Motor Show 34,000. In isolation, not comparable to the nearly half a million visitors to an Earls Court show, but then that tally took ten days to achieve and for carmakers Goodwood visitors were far more likely to be customers.

FAREWELL EARLS COURT

As the traditional British motor show was declining, the final curtain of Earls Court itself beckoned.

In 2007 the Earls Court and Olympia Group (ECO Venues) announced a 50:50 joint venture agreement with Capital & Counties (Capco) to own and manage Earls Court and Olympia exhibition centres plus the Chiswell Street Brewery venue. The stated aim was to establish the venues 'as landmark leisure destinations, centred around the core businesses of exhibitions, conferences and special events'.

In 2008 it bought a 50 per cent stake in the Empress Building, the 1960s office block built on the site of the Empress Hall and the remaining stake of the exhibition centre in January 2010, giving it the ability to build on the land. It was becoming clear that the

From the air, c. 2007: Warwick Road entrance lower left, Earls Court 2 crosses the lines and fills what was once a car park. The tower block is the Empress Building, on the site of the Empress Hall. See chapter 1 for the 1937 shot. (Olympia)

The swimming pool reveals itself to be in fairly good shape at 70 years old in 2007. See chapter 1 for its creation. (Olympia)

1930s building's days might be numbered, even though it was fully active and due to play host to the Olympic volleyball tournament in summer 2012.

A Capco spokesman told BBC online that, 'In terms of the venue, no final decisions have been taken,' but added, 'We are presently exploring the option of an enhancement of our world class exhibition centre at Olympia rather than replacing the current exhibition centre at Earls Court.'

Paul Colston, managing editor of Exhibition News website, said, 'There's a £22bn events industry in the UK and this is a real blow. London will be losing its flagship exhibition venue in the UK. This will hurt the whole industry because it's the flagship exhibition venue and not easily replaceable.'

In May 2010 Capco, with Transport for London (TfL) and the London Borough of Hammersmith & Fulham, announced that the well-known architects Terry Farrell & Partners would work with them to draw up a master plan for the Earls Court site. This would include an 'in-depth community and stakeholder consultation'

with local residents, and the council would decide if it wanted to include the West Kensington and Gibbs Green housing estates in the development area.

The following March the scheme went out for public consultation and in June planning applications for the 'Earls Court & West Kensington Opportunity Area' were submitted.

The outline application for the 77-acre site included the exhibition centre, two housing estates plus a further detailed application for the 7.5-acre Seagrave Road car park site. It was stated to have a total estimated value of £8 billion, creating 7,500 new homes and 12,000 new jobs. There would be new offices, leisure, hotel and retail space, a new primary school, library, health centre and 23.5 acres of public open space including a 5-acre 'Lost River Park' opening up Counters Creek. Approved by both Hammersmith & Fulham and Kensington borough councils in 2012, the massive scheme is said to take twenty years to fully complete.

There was loud local opposition, both to the loss of the venue and the overall redevelopment. The Earls Court Area Action Group

The 'deconstruction' of Earls Court was a massive project started in January 2015. Left to right: Earls Court 2 dominates the landscape in June; seen from Old Brompton Road, the roof has nearly gone by September and the Warwick Road entrance, shorn of its signage, is barely visible. (Author's collection)

called it an 'utterly inappropriate designer ghetto [that] will contain no affordable housing' which would put great strain on local roads and Underground stations.

Nonetheless, in July 2013 Boris Johnson, Mayor of London, gave it the final green light.

Although London buildings such as Battersea Power Station and Smithfield Market had been redeveloped with some of their architecture preserved, hopes that at least the façade of the Earls Court Exhibition Centre might be retained were dashed when English Heritage deemed it not interesting enough to gain listed status. '[We] did not recommend Earls Court Exhibition Centre for listing as it lacked architectural interest and many of the original features had been lost,' English Heritage's planning and conservation director, Nigel Barker, told *City AM*.

In July 2014 the 'Deconstruction Process' of Earls Court 1 and 2 was published. Demolition had moved well away from swinging a ball at a building to a painstakingly planned dismantling so as not to affect the surrounding areas and to handle harmful materials such as asbestos (present in much of Earls Court's roofing). Six stages would dismantle Earls Court 2 apart from the concrete slab over the West London line and bring Earls Court 1 down to its basement slab by summer 2016.

The last car-themed event ever to be held at Earls Court was a lavish evening launch for the new Jaguar XE in September 2014. On 14 December the last ever Earls Court show was a performance by the Bombay Bicycle Club, a North London band. By January 2015 the 'deconstruction' hoardings were up.

Olympia, the 'village hall' that Earls Court had been built to supplant, had emphatically survived it, a £45 million refurbishment taking it into the 130th year since its foundations were laid by the Earl of Zetland.

BIBLIOGRAPHY

Akhtar, Miriam and Humphries, Steve. *The Fifties and Sixties: A Lifestyle Revolution* (Boxtree, 2001).

Baldwin, Nick; Georgano, Nick; Clausager, Anders; Wood, Jonathan. *Britain's Motor Industry: The First Hundred Years* (G.T. Foulis & Co., 1995).

Bobbitt, Malcolm. *The British Citroën* (Transport Publishing Company, 1991).

Bunton, Nigel. *A History of Electric Cars* (Crowood Press, 2013).

Chapman, Giles. *Cars We Loved in the 1970s* (The History Press, 2013).

Church, Roy. *The Rise and Decline of the British Motor Industry* (Cambridge University Press, 1995).

Daniels, Jeff. *British Leyland: The Truth about the Cars* (Osprey Publishing Ltd, 1980).

Georgano, Nick (compiler). *The Complete Encyclopaedia of Motorcars: 1885 to the Present* (Ebury Press, 1982).

Glanfield, John. *Earls Court and Olympia: From Buffalo Bill to the 'Brits'* (Sutton Publishing, 2003).

Hayes, Russell. *Ford Cortina: The Complete History* (Haynes Publishing, 2012).

Hayes, Russell. *Lotus: The Creative Edge* (Haynes Publishing, 2007).

Hayes, Russell. *TVR: Ever the Extrovert* (Haynes Publishing, 2009).

Pressnell, Jon. *Austin Healey: The Bulldog Breed* (Haynes Publishing, 2011).

Pressnell, Jon. *Mini: The Definitive History* (Haynes Publishing, 2009).

Pressnell, Jon. *Morris: The Cars and the Company* (Haynes Publishing, 2013).

Pullen, Stephen. *British Leyland: From Steam Wagons to Seventies Strife* (Heritage Commercials, 2011).

Sedgwick, Michael; Gillies, Mark. *A–Z of Cars, 1945–1970* (Haymarket Publishing, 1986).

Voller, David J. *British Cars of the Early Sixties, 1960–1964* (Compiled for the Olyslager Organisation). (Warne, 1981).

Magazine References

Autocar/The Autocar (back issues).

Cardew, Basil. *Daily Express Motor Show Review, 1977 Cars* (Beaverbrook Newspapers, 1976).

Caverhill, Geoff. *Classic American*, August/September 2009 (Simpsons of Wembley).

Caverhill, Geoff. 'The Lendrum & Hartman Story', *Classic American*, June–July 2006.

Caverhill, Geoff. 'The Lincoln Cars Story', *Classic American*, February 2010.

Chapman, Giles. 'Prize Guys: The Daily Telegraph/IBCAM Styling Competition', *Classic and Sports Car*, October 1988.

Edwards, Jonathan. 'Show of Shows', *Classic and Sports Car*, November 1982 (Haymarket Publishing).

Motor (back issues).

Robson, Graham. 'Earls Court 1959', *Thoroughbred and Classic Cars*, December 1979 (IPC Transport Press).

Online resources

Buckley, Martin. 'Catching up with John Lennon's 140mph Iso Rivolta S4', www.telegraph.co.uk, 27 November 2004.

Chapman, Giles. 'British Motor Show: Golden Years', www.telegraph.co.uk, 25 July 2008.

Gardner, Bill. 'Luxury Limousine that Nearly Brought Down Daimler to Go Under the Hammer', www.telegraph.co.uk, 10 September 2014.

www.britishpathe.com. (Marvellous Motor Show clips.)

www.motor sportmagazine.com. (Thanks to *Motorsport* magazine for having scanned a great deal of its past issues and made them available on the web.)

www.olympia.co.uk.

www.thisismoney.co.uk. (Money conversions using annual RPI inflation 2014.)